The

BUSIN
PROCESS
RE-ENGINEERING
action kit

**A FIVE DAY
PLAN TO
REDESIGN YOUR
PROCESSES**

Michael Ballé

**KOGAN
PAGE**

YOURS TO HAVE AND TO HOLD
BUT NOT TO COPY

First published in 1995

Kogan Page Limited
120 Pentonville Road
London N1 9JN

© Michael Ballé, 1995

British Library Cataloguing in Publication Data

A CIP record for this book is available from the British Library.

Typeset by Books Unlimited (Nottm), Mansfield NG19 7QZ
Printed in England by Clays Ltd, St Ives plc

CONTENTS

ACKNOWLEDGEMENTS

———————— ✧ ————————

As I was working on practical applications of the Systems Thinking framework[1], I came across Michael Hammer and James Champy's remarkable book *Re-engineering the Corporation: a Manifesto for Business Revolution*[2] which, in a way, established the programme for business process re-engineering. The concepts they exposed enabled me to draw a link between the general dynamic structures I had previously been studying, and the very pragmatic workplace improvement techniques I was using in practical applications. Reading their book started me thinking on presenting a practical approach within the programme they outlined. On the practical front, I would also like to thank Kiyoshi Suzaki for his ground-breaking work on shop-floor management[3] which has been a constant source of inspiration in my work with teams.

This book is the result of countless hours of workshops and working sessions. I cannot name all those who have helped me, through their enthusiasm and common sense, to put it all together, but I wish to thank most particularly Rachel Parr, Cindy Bull, Seema Shama, Laura George, Cheryl Sheard, Peter Smith and Richard Talbot for working with me in making it all work in practice. I also want to thank Jean Cox, Michel Marissal and Alain Prioul for teaching me how to see processes in action on the shop-floor. Special thanks to my father, Freddy Ballé, whose in-depth knowledge and experience of these matters provided clear and insightful advice; and to Robert Abbott, Andrew Gottschalk, Richard Hervey, and Michael Kightley for their friendship and support. Many thanks to Philip Mudd for his thoughtful editorial guidance and Rosemary Bennett for her skilful editing. Finally, last but never least, I am grateful to my wife, Lisa Ballé, for her constant support and good sense.

1. Ballé, M (1994) *Managing with Systems Thinking*, McGraw-Hill, Maidenhead.
2. Hammer, M & Champy, J (1993) *Re-engineering the Corporation*, Harper Collins, New York.
3. Suzaki, K (1993) *The New Shop Floor Management*, The Free Press, New York.

For Lisa, with all my love

INTRODUCTION

✧

PROCESS REDESIGN: WHAT IS IT? WHO NEEDS IT? WHY SHOULD YOU BOTHER?

Business Process Re-engineering (BPR) has gathered momentum to the point where almost everyone in business is talking about 'processes' or 're-engineering'. Yet, as the BPR movement picks up speed, it is also drawn into a polemic about how 'effective' it is, about what results it gets. All in all, the scope one can give to the concept is so large that people can read more or less what they want into it. For some it means restructuring, for others 'downsizing', or 'strategic re-focus' of their organisations. And as more people join the band wagon, it becomes increasingly difficult to know how to feel about re-engineering, and more importantly about what to do in practice.

Beyond the hype, BPR is fundamentally about redesigning processes. The scope for process redesign can range from the widest restructure of the entire organisation, to the most local rethink about how you do your own work. The main underlying issue is that of practical organisation of work: for complex outputs to be achieved, a number of sequential tasks needs to be done, which usually involves co-ordinating a variety of people. The sequencing of tasks and co-ordination of people to do them is an issue as old as organisations themselves. Each decade brings its new solution, and with it, its new problems. Re-engineering is the answer to the over-complexity and hyper-specialisation brought by the tremendous development of large organisations in the 1960s and 1970s. The main idea is to try to get back to some simpler way of organising, which will actually make sense from a *work* point of view.

A worthy and necessary aim, taking into account the general toughening of the business environment and the administrative productivity crisis firms are facing today, but how do we achieve it? Much has been written on the subject, but very little of the BPR literature can be applied immediately. Most of the time, it tells you how bad things are and how things should be, but remains vague about how to get there from here. In this book, I have tried to focus on the how, and to present a number of directly applicable techniques which can be used right away!

In this respect, this book is written for practical-minded managers who know what problems they have and are looking for practical ways to go forward. There are no miracle solutions, and if you want to re-engineer your business processes, sooner or later you will have to go down to grassroots level where the work is actually being done. For those who are willing to get their hands dirty and grapple with the messy, complex and somewhat baffling nature of real organisational situations, this book offers methods, techniques as well as practical hints and tips to deal with real-life issues. In the Questions and Answers section, I have also tried to address more formal issues about business processes, which are a necessary complement to the practical chapters for a complete understanding.

Why bother? Because at the end of the day, organisations take up a lot of our lives, and improving working environments is well worth the effort. As competitive pressures increase, there is a temptation to transfer this pressure to people — to get them to work longer, faster, harder. Though this solution can work in the short-term, it is in no way sustainable. And with alienated staff, burned-out managers and anxious, embattled directors, the firm still has to face an outside pressure which is not letting up. The problem is not working harder, but working smarter. The pressure is real, but we must remember that an organisation can compete only through the motivation and competence — the will and skill — of the people in it. To turn the competitive pressure into advantage we must work with our staff and find ways to instil their intelligence in our working practices, rules and hierarchies.

In a sense, this is what I have attempted to do with this book. I have summarised the insight of many people — professionals, consultants, academics — and formatted it in a practical, easy-to-implement form. Certainly, I have outlined pragmatic 'tips', but mostly, this book presents a way of using the intelligence of the people who are doing the actual work. Through workshops and on the job, their experience and insight can be shared and forged into pragmatic, mutually beneficial solutions. In order to do this, I have taken the approach of being tough on the problem, not on the people. The techniques rely on everyone's professional competence and expertise rather than traditional 'team spirit' pressures. If there is a general lesson to be drawn from BPR, I believe that it is in the necessity to move away from 'command-and-control' organisations, and progressively, rebuild organisations on the strength of collective and collaborative intelligence.

PROCESS REDESIGN: THE TECHNIQUES BEHIND RE-ENGINEERING AND PROCESS IMPROVEMENT

———————— ✦ ————————

Consider:

> You are on the board of a company and you learn through the grapevine that its main competitor is about to 're-engineer' its entire operation ...

Or:

> You are a department head in a large company and you've just heard that top management has decided to 're-engineer' the company in order to get more 'customer-focused' ...

What do you do? First there was TQM, then JIT and now comes BPR! Business Process Re-engineering has spread like wildfire in North American and European companies since the late 1980s. Is it here to stay? Or is it one of those managerial crazes which sweep through the business world every five to ten years? We are all aware of the weakness that top management has for neatly packaged solutions, peddled by slick consultants. Seasoned managers tend to rely on one of the following three strategies to survive these great moments of organisational change:

Keep your head down!

With any luck it will go away, just like One-Minute Managing, Corporate Culture Change, Entrepreneurship or 'Excellence'. Not a bad strategy as long as there isn't a real problem to deal with in the first place. Of course, if there *is* a real crisis, chances are that the 'ostrich strategy' will lead to disaster.

If you can't beat them, join them

It's for real: young, earnest consultants with impeccable bedside manners are appearing all over the place to re-engineer the company. Maybe there is something in it for you if you join one of the redesign teams?

Large consultancies have both the expertise and the experience to conduct full-scale re-engineering efforts. Unfortunately, they often have two serious draw-backs:

- They are very expensive (in terms of large outlays of cash).
- They tend to focus on high-level analysis and seldom actually get down to task level where the root of the problem is.

Do it yourself!

Why not? Most of these fashions tend to be based on a few fundamental good points. What is it about re-engineering that your own team cannot understand or implement? If you feel that your company does not have all the expertise in-house, why not hire independent consultants for specific tasks, such as running workshops? Process re-engineering is first and foremost about common sense on top of an inside-out understanding of the mechanics of the business. In this sense, front-line managers are the best people to re-engineer their own processes. All they need is a method. We will try to provide this in the book.

A SERIOUS ISSUE: MANAGEMENT PRODUCTIVITY

There is a fundamental issue underlying all the hype about business re-engineering: our organisations are definitely getting bogged down under their own weight. As Peter Drucker[1] points out, the productivity problem in the agricultural sector—which has dogged humanity since the Neolithic revolution—has been solved. Less than 5 per cent of the active population can now complete the work which used to involve almost everybody. Agricultural production has been transformed by extensive use of mechanisation, following industrial revolution. In fact, productivity increases in production have also been astounding since the turn of the century. As the end of the twentieth century approaches, most people work in the 'services' sector. Yet, in this area, productivity is actually declining!

Organisations have become so large and unwieldy that they require hordes of people to run their administrative, informational and control systems. For each customer served, how many accountants, computer wizards, and managers of all sorts? The way we build our giant organisations is now counter-productive. This productivity problem also turns out to be a major competitive issue in a global economy.

George Stalk and Thomas Hout[2] from the BCG present the following example. They compared the staff structure of two competing automotive parts suppliers in the US.

	US Firm	Japanese Firm
Volume (pa)	10 M	3.5 M
Product Types	11	38
Units per Worker	43 100	61 400
Staff		
Direct	107	50
Support	135	7
Total	242	57
Cost per Unit	$100	$49

This example shows a striking difference from a classic American mass production strategy to a more flexible, process-focused Japanese strategy. If the difference in productivity is striking, the difference in overhead is even more so.

Business process re-engineering tries to address the productivity issue. Behind all the hype, modern companies are faced with a painful and complex problem: the way they traditionally build organisations no longer works.

BUSINESS PROCESS RE-ENGINEERING: DOES IT WORK?

It does. Of course, BPR is not a magical solution. Not all attempts get good results. Nevertheless, the evidence is largely positive. A large-scale study from CSC index[3] in 1994 shows that:

1. 60 per cent of the 497 North American companies sampled had

engaged in at least one re-engineering exercise; as had 75 per cent of the 124 European companies interrogated.

2. Most companies had concrete results to show for their efforts. Some objectives appear harder to reach than others. Less than half the companies aiming for an increase in market share were satisfied in that respect. However, most companies seeking to lower their costs had satisfying results and three-quarters of companies intending to reduce lead-time and increase productivity achieved their objectives.

When confronted with the reality of operations, it is often difficult to know what to make of each new thing that comes from the West—or the East, for that matter. Large corporations tend to embrace these various fashions with abandon, only to hit snags two or three years down the line. Very soon, as the trend gathers momentum, it also gets seriously questioned from a variety of sources. Typically, on the face of uneven results, consultants will blame some form of 'managerial resistance to change'. Middle-management makes a good target since most of us are unclear about who middle-management is exactly. This failure-due-to-resistance explanation can be rather surprising considering that management attitudes should be taken into account in any change project in the first place. Such rash blame allocation can make any technique unpopular very quickly. Eventually the entire approach tends to be discredited, and management looks for the next miracle solution. Unfortunately, the real problem does not disappear by simply discarding a disappointing solution.

THE TECHNIQUES UNDERLYING MANAGERIAL TRENDS

This is how *The Economist*[4] describes the re-engineering movement:

> Re-engineering is a management mongrel. On the one side its ancestors are Japanese theories about lean, flexible, just-in-time production; on the other, American ones about redesigning companies from the bottom up. In essence, BPR argues that to remain competitive, companies should forget about the old practice of dividing themselves into bureaucratic empires, focused on discrete tasks, such as sales, marketing and accounts, and instead organise around continuous business processes, aimed at getting the product to the customer.

As with most things, it is important to distinguish the true value of any new method from the headlines it generates. Earlier, we mentioned TQM and JIT. Although the trend element may have passed, their core teachings remain as valid today as they were ten years ago. Focused quality policies and low stock production have become absolute prerequisites in many industries. TQM and JIT are founded on very valid practices which companies need to implement in order to remain competitive, particularly in industry branches competing with Japan.

It is noteworthy that many of these managerial dogmas of the 1980s were originally developed in Japan as shop-floor level techniques. Imported to the US, they get transformed into large-scale organisational models. Statistical quality control becomes Total Quality Management. The Just-in-Time production system (which is mostly about manufacturing, product flows, batch sizes and tool change-overs) becomes the Lean Enterprise. And, similarly, practical work on processes becomes Business Re-engineering. In Europe, when we finally hear about these things from the US, they have become generic concepts which should help CEOs to radically transform their entire organisations. This inflating of technical concepts is probably necessary to their diffusion.

At the root of TQM, Quality Circles, *Kaizen* and so forth, the Japanese and their Western spokesmen have preached for an emphasis on *process rather than task*. Continuous improvement is about continuously improving the value-adding processes in the company. From that point of view, if we focus on strict value-adding to the firm's products or services we immediately realise that many of the middle-hierarchy or administrative operations have nothing to do with it. These layers of work happen for internal reasons, not because they add any value to the products or services. Through rationalising these processes, firms have been able to considerably lower their administrative or support overhead.

HOW FAR SHOULD YOU GO IN 'RE-ENGINEERING' YOUR COMPANY?

Re-engineering often demands radical organisational changes. It considers 'functional' organisation to be the source of all corporate evils—but is it really the case? The basic idea is that large (or small) organisations develop around functions, ie Production, Sales, Finance, Marketing etc. These functions have their own hierarchies, their specialists, their techniques and even, to a certain extent, their own cultures. Functions have emerged as a consequence of various historical and practical reasons, but the bottom line is that they don't really 'make sense':

To get a product to the customer you have to:

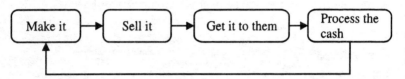

Of course, the more of this you do, the more complex it becomes. Instead of doing it all yourself, suddenly you end up with Making It specialists, Selling It specialists, Getting It To Them specialists and Money specialists. All those specialists have now special needs, which tend to generate a further level of specialism. Selling generates Marketing; Marketing generates R&D and Production and Quality Control and so on; and as for money, well, there is no end to the professions one can invent under that topic.

So, all of a sudden, you end up with something quite awkward to manage, with hierarchies developing in each of the branches and so forth.

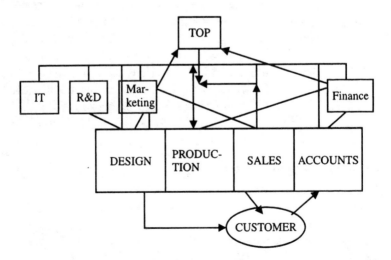

The original flow, ie sequence of actions, still has to be maintained. But now this sequence is greatly complicated by having to deal with:

- All these different people.
- Their territorial issues.
- And the general complexity of organisational life.

Business re-engineering's fundamental idea is to somehow re-organise the company according to its few fundamental workflows. This, of course, entails breaking down the functions and their hierarchies.

SHOULD WE GET RID OF FUNCTIONAL ORGANISATIONS?

As we progressively learn from on-going business re-engineering experiments, we find that functional organisation has a role to play in modern structures. Indeed, as J Womack, D Jones and D Roos, authors of *The Machine that Changed the World*[5] point out, to work optimally, organisational design must take three driving factors into account:

The needs of the organisation

To be competitive on the market, the organisation's processes must be fully functional. Companies therefore need to control where and how the value is added at each step of their internal processes. This usually means breaking down the functional chimneys and moving people around the organisation.

The needs of the function

Functions represent expertise and knowledge centres—and need to be developed as such. Too general a manager will lose touch with the level of narrow expertise that is needed to compete on each segment of the value chain.

The needs of the individual

Individuals need to see clear career paths which recognise their expertise. They also need to work within groups where their specific expertise can be appreciated, rewarded and enhanced. A process manager will find it difficult to survive in any political organisational context.

WHERE DO FUNCTIONAL ORGANISATIONS COME FROM?

In a way, *nothing fails like success*. The work organisation at the very root of our industrial revolution has been followed up to such an extreme that it has now turned against us. For almost two centuries, labour has been organised around Adam Smith's insight about fragmenting work into its component tasks. In itself, the idea is simple (revolutionary at the time): several highly specialised workers performing single elementary tasks would produce more efficiently than the same number of generalists each engaged in performing the whole work. In practice, this notion was to structure manufacturing for over two centuries. Its advantages are outlined by Adam Smith in *The Wealth of Nations*[6] published in 1776:

> This great increase of the quantity of work which, in consequence of the division of labour, the same number of people are capable of performing, is owing to three different circumstances; first, to increase the dexterity in every particular workman; secondly, to the saving of the time which is commonly lost in passing from one species of work to another; and lastly, to the invention of a great number of machines which facilitate and abridge labour, and enable one man to do the work of many.

This is important to understand, first because the productivity impact of specialisation of tasks was tremendous, and second, because the process issues Smith outlined are still dogging us today. These are:

- Individual expertise or competence.
- Time lost in passing from one piece of work to another, or from one working station to the next—let alone from one functional department to the next.
- Automating (whether with machine-tools or computers).

The principle of fragmenting tasks to their elementary components was later brought to the height of refinement by Frederick Taylor in his *Principles of Scientific Management*[7] where each task was 'scientifically' optimised by an engineer and performed by an unskilled worker. It was then successfully applied in industry by Henry Ford who created the first modern manufacturing plants. In fact, this concept was to be further developed by Alfred Sloan at General Motors who applied it to *management*.

To cope with the increasing complexity of the growing auto man-ufacturing business, Sloan split general management into areas of *specialisation* such as Production, Marketing, Finance and so forth. His understanding was that a manager didn't need to know the details of operations as long as he had a clear understanding of the financial figures to keep his business 'in line'. In doing so, he set a model which led to most of the problems re-engineering is trying to deal with today. We are now aware of the numerous drawbacks these original solutions have had through the years. Yet, it is important to understand the *logic* of such structures. In effect, once you fragment work into elementary tasks, you also need to build hierarchies to supervise these tasks and to co-ordinate at a higher level in order to finally come up with a finished product.

Evidently, the breaking down of processes into individual tasks is mostly arbitrary. The tremendous productivity improvements gained at the manufacturing level are off-set by wide-spread costs at a more general organisational level: a product must still be processed from beginning to end and supplied to the customer. There is an overall cost to functional inefficiency which comprises:

■ Lack of communication.
■ Co-ordination complexities.
■ Decision-making delays.
■ Territorial political fights.
■ Overgrown hierarchies.

Traditionally, this cost was not a problem inasmuch as it wouldn't be charged to any specific department. It was however ultimately borne by the customer until three changes drastically modified the business environment:

Shift in power

As long as economies grew through consumers purchasing basic equip-ment (car, refrigerator, TV, etc), there was always more demand than offer, and the producer had the upper-hand: consumers had little choice but to take what was sold to them if they wanted the products at all. However, over the last decades, consumers have become more or less fully equipped, and producers now have to convince them to replace what they've got with something newer, better, cheaper. The balance of power has shifted from the producers to the consumers.

Global economy

In practice this means one doesn't compete with his or her best national neighbour (one or two firms at best) but with the best competitors from all over the world. Being better, faster, cheaper than your traditional neighbourly competitor is not much use if some outfit from South East Asia can undercut your products on your own markets.

The Toyota revolution

Japanese process-focused companies started competing with better quality, better service, faster development of new products and lower costs. The fundamental insight of the Toyota Production System was to use the benefits of mass production as developed by Ford, but to maintain an integrity of the processes throughout the company (which ultimately led to Cross-Functional Management). With this process focus, there is much less room for bureaucracies to develop, and even less overall organisational cost.

PROCESS RE-ENGINEERING AND CONTINUOUS IMPROVEMENT

In the early 1950s, several Japanese companies developed a drastically different way of looking at business processes, mainly because in the devastated state of their country, materials and machines were scarce. One of their major concerns was waste. Waste was an accepted aspect of American mass production, then in full swing. The Japanese engineers, however, simply could not afford waste—both in terms of product quality and process effectiveness. For instance, when Taiichi Ohno, Toyota's brilliant engineer, insisted on flexible machines rather than heavy dedicated ones, he explains that, back in the 1950s, they could barely afford a few machines. They certainly didn't have the money for dedicated heavy investment. When American quality specialists presented their work to Japanese engineers they immediately recognised the framework, tools and techniques they were looking for, and thus planted the seeds of the 'Quality Revolution' which would challenge Western industries decades later.

As they were struggling in the face of impossible odds, a few Japanese companies came up with the notion of continuous improvement (or *Kaizen*). Continuous improvement is quite different from our traditional approach to progress because it does not necessarily call for a large investment. However, it does call for a great deal of continuous effort and commitment. The difference between the two opposing concepts can be likened to that of a staircase and a slope. The innovation strategy is supposed to bring about progress in staircase progression as depicted:

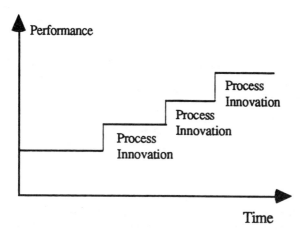

Continuous improvement brings about gradual progress. It turns out that this continual approach is very powerful because the classical 'step change' strategy is, in practice, not quite as effective as it sounds. Instead of following the staircase pattern, the actual progress achieved through innovation will generally follow the pattern shown below.

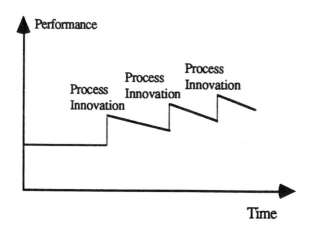

Without being complemented with continuous improvement, innovation keeps slipping back to former levels of productivity. This happens because a system, once it has been installed as a result of new innovation, is subject to steady deterioration unless continuing efforts are made first to maintain it, then to improve it.

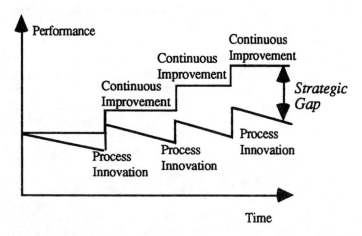

Intuitively, it is reasonable to assume that anything 'left to itself' will steadily deteriorate, and most of us have witnessed brilliant innovation slowly dissolve in the corporate mess.

Apart from the obvious benefits of maintaining a continuous improvement effort on corporate processes, this attitude raises another significant organisational issue: the locus of control is shifted down the hierarchy. Because of the usually large investment required by innovation, the decision-making and action-power can usually be found in the nebulous strata of upper-management. The front-line people hear that they will be provided with a new system and had better get on with it. When this doesn't work out, they can all blame organisational inertia or resistance to change.

In the case of continuous improvement, action and decision-making is located *on the shop-floor*. The responsibility for improvement is no longer only in the hierarchy, but also, very practically, in the hands of the workers themselves. That obvious shift has wide-ranging implications in companies that are structured to specifically avoid any initiative at shop-floor level!

BUSINESS RE-ENGINEERING

Business re-engineering is, in a way, the Western answer to continuous improvement. The contention of its advocates is that whereas process focus is essential, most Western firms are not yet ready to go the continuous improvement route. To be able to do so, a firm needs to be already process oriented. Business re-engineering proposes to do away with the old dysfunctional, fragmented processes and specialised structures and to re-design corporations according to better adapted rules. In the words of M Hammer and J Champy, the consultants who coined the expression 'business re-engineering':

> When someone asks us for a quick definition of business re-engineering, we say that it means 'starting over', it doesn't mean tinkering with what already exists or making incremental changes that leave basic structures intact. It isn't about making patchwork fixes—jury-rigging existing systems so that they work better. It does mean abandoning long-established procedures and looking afresh at the work required to create a company's product or service and deliver value to the customer. It means asking this question: 'If I were re-creating this company today, given what I know and given current technology, what would it look like?'[8]

Although business re-engineering expounds a rather different philosophical attitude to change than does continuous improvement, one perhaps more adapted to the American 'hero culture', several of its basic tenets are very similar to Japanese continuous improvement approaches. The changes involved, however, are considerable.

Focus on business processes rather than functional tasks

The organisational consequence is that people's roles change from 'controlled to empowered'. In a task-oriented company, faithful to the Taylorian ideal, managers will hire people and expect them to behave according to set rules.

Delegate decision-making to the workplace

A re-engineered company places the emphasis on working processes and therefore moves the decision-making power to employees and teams. For it to work, decisions need to be taken in real time at the workplace.

Empower teams

As management invests teams with the responsibility of completing entire processes, it also needs to give them the authority to make the appropriate decisions and commitments. This bypasses the traditional painstaking process of getting approval from the hierarchy for any slight change in the organisation of work.

FINDING THE MIDDLE PATH

In fact, each approach brings its own very practical problems to the European manager. On the one hand, business re-engineering is very seductive because of the sheer scope intended. Top managers can think, 'hang on, here is a great solution to overhaul my entire business and gain the leading edge.' But, in practice, experience shows that many full scale re-engineering efforts have disappointing results. Blame is mostly allocated two ways: 'lack of top management commitment' on the one hand, and 'resistance to change' from staff on the other. The truth is that such massive endeavours are actually quite risky simply because of the sheer size of the projects involved.

Furthermore, there is a particular danger in full scale re-engineering: it is easy to fall back into classical 're-organisation'. At the end of the day, if we restructure along classical lines, all we have done is change the names in the boxes, and maybe the arrangement of the boxes themselves, but very little has changed *at task level*. A clear symptom that this sort of thing is happening is when the centralise–decentralise debate appears. Another form of this debate is market focused–product focused organisations. Product focus becomes market focus, or vice-versa—shedding staff in the process.

A blue-chip company recently went through a total re-engineering led by one of the major consultancies. After hours of interviews, months of delays, and a considerable amount of personal traumas, the new structure was announced. Originally, the company had been organised according to product lines. The re-engineered structure would be organised by geographical regions in order to be 'closer to the customers'. This new structure mostly affected management levels and rarely touched upon physical workflows. On the shop-floor, cynical employees who had been with the company long enough to know better chuckled as they confided that regional organisation was how the company was ten years ago, before it was organised by product lines within an 'excellency' drive to 'stick to the knitting'.

These sort of changes might not be unhealthy in terms of competitive advantage and strategy, but are they worth the cost, both in financial and human terms? At process level, such restructuring makes very little difference because the work (ie succession of tasks) still has to be done, regardless of who's the boss. If the tasks themselves haven't been focused on, all we have really changed is the internal power structure of the company—not its effectiveness.

PROCESS REDESIGN

Most consultants will argue that one has to 'go big'. The larger the scope of the re-engineering projects, the bigger the gains (and the fees). This visionary approach tends to ignore the fact that the larger the scope, the more difficulties one is likely to encounter. Redesigning processes does not need to challenge outright the organisational structure. There is no reason why processes could not be improved one at a time. The likelihood is that as we go on redesigning processes we will sooner or later question the organisational structure. But this will then be an informed challenge—not an ideological debate about the 'functional chimneys'. It will also be specific enough to find practical solutions to whatever problems arise.

Department level

Redesign can occur at department level: workflows are improved on a team-to-team basis. However, the total functional structure of the company is not challenged. The organisation chart is modified only inasmuch as operational changes require obvious organisational changes. The work remains focused on a step-by-step approach and major changes are recommended only after having been thoroughly tested in practice.

Operational focus

The focus is operational: the processes are examined at task level, and any changes made involve task re-arrangements. Organisational issues are taken into consideration only when they affect task co-ordination. This gives us a very pragmatic and practical outlook about how work is done. The question is not about what *should* work, but what *does* work.

Team-based

If we deal with operational problems, we need to use team-based techniques because those who actually *do* the job have to be present. The broad, wide-scale re-engineering effort can afford to stay in management boardrooms and 'redesign' the organisations on paper, or on the basis of interview results. This, however, will never be a true reflection of the operational reality of work. Operational means 'I do this, then I do that, then I send it all to her, who does this and so forth.' The collective dimension is a necessity to capture the practicality of people's actions.

WORKFLOWS

Fundamentally, processes are about workflows, ie flows of work. From an operational perspective, any 'work' is a series of actions which happen in sequence. If these actions are related, the sequence constitutes a flow. Our problem will be quite simply to render these flows as effective as possible. Process redesign is about:

- Understanding what a process is.
- Mapping process workflows.
- Improving workflows in processes.

As we do this progressively throughout a department or a company, we start to take control of our own organisation. First by understanding it from an operational perspective, and second by improving it brick by brick.

In effect, the process redesign approach makes the link between continuous improvement and full-scale business re-engineering. Both approaches—when not used by their developers—lead to practical problems when we try to apply them. The *Kaizen* approach tends to drive specific, practical improvements which are then hard to generalise, whilst the re-engineering approach can end up being a classical reorganisation (reshuffling of the hierarchy) and does not get down to task level. The process redesign approach takes an in-between road between those two extremes.

WHERE IS THE VALUE ADDED?

The guiding principle in our efforts is to identify the value added—and cut out the rest. Value-added can only be determined by the customers: what are they happy to pay for? In redesigning our processes, we shall try to minimise non-value tasks. Where is the value-added? Value-added is contained in those few actions we do that actually *add value* to the product or service we provide to our customer (the next person in the process, in fact). The rest is waste. Would you be willing to pay for the cost of 'work-in-progress' stocks, transportation, or waiting-time included in a product if you had any other alternative? Anything we can't legitimately charge our customer for should be considered as waste. The first step of getting organised is then to hunt waste systematically and without mercy. Hunting waste is not a one-off operation, it is an attitude.

Wasting work

'Wasting work' is doing too much that is not actually useful. We sometimes go into too much detail, or over-engineer the things which matter to us (or that we know how to do well) but that the customer doesn't greatly care about—such as five decimal digits in forecasting. The other type of wasted work is all the useless things we have to go through because of complex administrative procedures, or involved processes, but which stop us from doing our real work.

Wasting time

Have you ever been stuck in a queue at a railway station waiting to buy a ticket for a train which is departing in 5 minutes, with the person in front of you arguing (for the past half hour) for a reimbursement of his ticket? The railways could make the difference between short (and possibly urgent) tasks and long and complex ones. Badly organised processes often result in wasting time not only for those who do the work but also for the customer (the next person in the process). In the example of the train ticket, the process is not about selling tickets but about getting people on the train!

Wasted transportation

In most working processes we waste an incredible amount of time and effort carrying things around; looking for things and shuffling them here and there—think about how many miles you cover just by carrying files from one meeting room to another!

Wasted inventory

Some people feel happy only if they have a large in-tray because it proves they're desperately busy. This is wasted inventory. Each task that is stuck in an in-tray somewhere is *costing money*! Obviously, inventory is much more costly in a production process—but the folder that is waiting on your desk for too long might push the customer to give up on it and try his or her luck elsewhere.

Defects

Defects are probably the most critical waste. Particularly so with complex projects, the later they appear the more expensive they are to rectify. So, rather than doing something badly, don't do it.

ONE PROCESS AT A TIME

At the end of the day we are indeed trying to re-establish some kind of process integrity. In a factory, it is reasonably easy. One can physically follow a product from A to B and then move machines and workstations around so that work happens uninterruptedly from beginning to end for each product. For other more administrative processes this can be far more difficult because:

- There is no obvious 'product' to follow.
- The tasks themselves are often far less defined than in a factory.
- Work efficiency has rarely been studied in offices as relentlessly

as it has on the factory shop-floor, so there is usually less methodological expertise to draw upon.

The greatest time waster of all is interruption, ie stopping task A in order to get ahead with task B, and then coming back to task A. The greatest source of errors is interruption. We tend to forget things easily between the moment we put A down, and pick it up again. If one person starts A and the next finishes it, then the risk of error grows exponentially, due to the fact that we seldom communicate all the facts to the other person. Even if we pick up the work ourselves, we are more than likely to have forgotten what it's all about. All in all an efficient and robust process is one where work happens uninterrupted from start to finish. This might not always be practical, but, as a guiding principle, this is what we should always try to achieve.

2

RE-ENGINEERING A PROCESS

The aim of process redesign is to provide a method to improve processes in practice, with the least disruption of work and with the fastest operational results as possible. The approach is based on the following principles:

- *Team based*: the techniques take advantage of collective experience of the practicalities of work.
- *Practical*: every action is based on practical necessity rather than intellectual theorising.
- *Live*: the work happens on live processes.
- *Results oriented*: at the end of the day, the process is evaluated by the customers of its output.

In order to improve their processes in practice, companies need a pragmatic method to coach their teams through process improvement. This is what I will try to describe here. In further sections, I will justify more fully these 'recipes' from a theoretical point of view. In the present context, however, the aim is to present in a practical format a usable framework. By following the framework step-by-step, any team should be able to successfully redesign its processes.

TIMESCALES

Experience shows that the least disruptive method for tackling process improvement is to work on one process at a time. First, the other processes can adapt to the changes; secondly, it is easier to control what we are doing—and to evaluate it; thirdly, we can benefit from the learning that occurred with previous processes. The process redesign framework itself takes about five days to run through a process:

Day 1

Placing an order for the output from the process and interviewing end-customers about their *use* of these outputs (how do these outputs fit within their own processes?).

Day 2

Walking through the process to get an idea of its route and number of steps. This enables the manager in charge to pick the relevant redesign team.

Days 3 and 4

Mapping the process and redesigning it. This is a full team day of work. It should be conducted in-house rather than off-site because the team might want to ask for information from their colleagues. The output for this day is a whiteboard presenting the new process to the organisation and set up to capture comments about its practicality.

On day four, *the comments are taken on board* and the process is finalised. An action plan is drawn for implementation and a board/form set up for customer comments.

Day 5

The team meets again at a later date (at least a month later) to evaluate its results and draw the appropriate lessons from their work.

If need be, the entire project can be run within one week. Experience shows that staff prefer meeting for one day at regular intervals, so as not to disrupt their work too much. This slower approach has the additional advantage of leaving everyone time to think. However, a two-day intensive workshop is necessary at the map and redesign stage. The process team needs to be protected from the pressures of day-to-day operations to be able to concentrate on the rather difficult task of redesigning the process on paper. A process could then be redesigned in a month, with one day a week working session—or any other arrangement.

It is also a good idea for the organisation to set up a regular process improvement programme which, although slower, is more steadfast rather than going for a more spectacular (and risky) exercise.

THE PROCESS REDESIGN FRAMEWORK

The 6-step framework can be outlined as follows.

Step 1: Order the Output

Before looking at the process, it is important to have a good under-standing of the output of this process—both actual and desired. 'Ordering' the output will help us to establish:

- The current form of the output.
- The trigger point to the process (customer order is the most obvious, but processes can have other trigger points, such as a date, or a manager's feeling that 'this hasn't been done for a long time' and so forth.)
- The average lead-time for the output to be produced.

Step 2: Sketch the process

In the second stage, we will sketch the process at a high level in order to:

- Establish the route followed by the work-in-process.
- Know who should be involved in the redesign team.
- Get an idea of the gap between lead-time and value-added time.

In practice, I have experimented with two different ways of conduct-ing this step, according to the complexity of the process.

The walk-through

The manager in charge of the area 'walks the order' through the process with the facilitation. At each workstation they ask the person responsible for the work to:

- Pick up the order and treat immediately.
- Explain what they are doing as they process the work.
- Indicate the next step.

Overall, this is probably the most effective way to outline a process. First, it will actually get done. Secondly, the manager can get a deep insight of how the process actually operates in practice. Thirdly, the manager shows to the staff that he or she is committed to the improvement effort. Finally, staff are gratified to spend some time demonstrating what they do to a member of management—and get a chance to think about problems and potential remedies.

On the other hand, if we are following a very complex or lengthy process, such an approach is not necessarily practical. In this case we shall use a different technique.

The tracer

By creating a physical file that moves through the process we can actually send a 'tracer' that will record:

■ in point and date;
■ work station;
■ task;
■ out point and date.

The information gathered in this way can then be collated to map the process.

Step 3: Mapping workflows

At this stage, the manager and facilitator can decide how to constitute the team so that it involves relevant members from each part of the process.

■ The team will then map out the entire process by describing on a Post-it each physical task that happens within their section. The notes will then be lined up on a whiteboard, and feedback loops drawn in with their decision rules.
■ The team will then identify entry points from other secondary processes.
■ The team will then inscribe lead-time and value-added time under each task step, as well as to point out any obvious discrepancy or inefficiency.

Step 4: Redesign the process

Once the process is actually mapped, the team will redesign it by following certain guidelines such as:

■ Eliminate entry or re-entry of data (by example change of system—as in shifting from one software to another within one process); automate any possible data entry (dates by example).
■ Reduce hand-offs from one person to another. This step might suggest organisational changes.
■ Separate work-items going through the process in terms of how

long they take to process. Special cases must be distinguished from routine jobs.

■ Negotiate with suppliers to the process for faster response (often the biggest lead-time increase factor).

The overall philosophy is quite straightforward: *simplify, simplify, simplify.*

Step 5: Check and test, test and check

Once the team has come up with what is considered a practical redesign and has presented it in task steps on a whiteboard, it must then invite all the persons concerned (staff, suppliers and customers) to comment on this design.

The idea is to have a whiteboard that is easily accessible to all the people in the hope that they will stop to read what's on it, and feel that they can make their own contribution in an informal manner. Comments should be invited, and written on the whiteboard as people pass. This is a critical part of achieving a successful implementation. Without following this step, many compatibility issues tend to go unnoticed. This phase also helps to communicate to the organisation that process work is under way and under control.

Once all the comments have been made the process is finalised by the team. The facilitator's presence is critical at this stage—some comments will be negative (ie 'it will never work because' type statements). The facilitator is needed to help the team take the practical part of these comments on board.

Step 6. Implementation and adjustments

The new process is now implemented. Several problems will appear; they are immediately written on the whiteboard. Another board is set up to enable the customers of the process to express their opinion (in an anonymous fashion if they wish). After a reasonable period of time, those comments are analysed by the team, built into the process and the process then finalised. This is done by writing a 'procedure', or in the process redesign programme terms, a 'best practice checklist'. Under each step (on the final whiteboard map of the process), the actual physical actions will be written by those who perform the tasks.

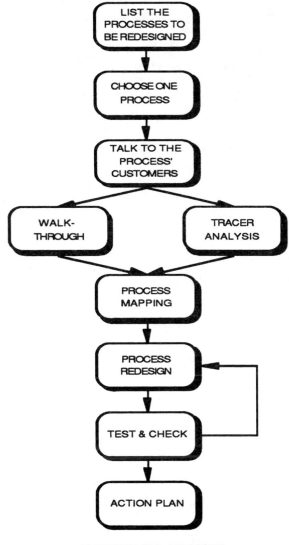

WHERE TO START?

When looking at an entire department or business, it is always difficult to find a starting point. Be practical: start with the area which gives you the most day-to-day hassle. It might not be the most clever place to start, but at least it will be easy to get commitment to do something about it. After one initial process has been designed, and the method has been experimented and is well in hand, we might want to start a systematic process redesign programme. We should then focus on the processes *close* to the customer. Once the processes closest to the customer are under control, we can then work upstream through the system to eventually redesign our entire operation.

3

STEP 1: ORDER THE OUTPUT

◇

To understand where the value is *actually* added in a process, one must place oneself in the customer's shoes. From this perspective, it is easy to judge what is value-added and what is simply 'moving about'.

Practical Tip: when looking at work, make the difference between movement and work. Many tasks involve energy without actual value-added work. Looking for a lost file is not work; moving materials from the depot to the plant is not work—it's movement.

The thing about customers is that they have no idea of what we go through to get them what they want—nor do they care. The customer's problem is to make a choice between different alternatives on the market, to make the purchase and use the product or service in the way he or she *likes*. It need not be the best way. It need not be the prescribed way. The customer will use your product in whatever way they have in mind. As a product or service provider, from the customer's point of view, *if you're not part of the solution, you're part of the problem*. Thankfully, most customers tend to be quite easygoing about their expectancies, or maybe they have no-where else to go so they don't mind waiting 20 minutes at the till for a £2 item. Still, it does not mean that they are happy about it. If a better alternative appears, you can bet they will complain with their feet: by walking over to your competitor.

However crucial, the interaction with the customer is only a small part of what the provider has to deal with. The provider must design the product or service, manufacture it, sell it, deal with accounts, design, advertising agencies and a thousand other things. Sometimes, the moment of truth with the customer might slip away from the attention of the provider's management.

For instance, suppose that you are a magazine publisher. You will have to deal with a surprising number of processes, such as:

- Getting articles for each publication.
- Creating new publications.
- Advertising for new subscribers.
- Registering new subscribers.
- Billing.
- Answering customer inquiries.
- Updating databases.
- Dealing with internal staff issues.
- Selling advertisement space.

Your customer's process is simply to choose which publication he or she is interested in, to subscribe, to pay and to read it!

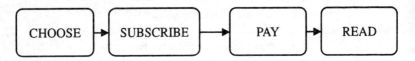

It is therefore understandable that although the value of your work should be defined by your customer, your real difficulties will come from internal problems. As we tend to focus on what gives us the most grief, the value of work has a natural tendency to slip away from the customer domain to being internally set. We do this because we think it is best. In itself, having a professional judgement on how things should be is what we get paid for, yet we run into serious trouble when our convenience is gained at the expense of value for the customer.

A very large Department Store was desperate to find ways of getting customers back. Throughout the 1980s, sales had consistently fallen as people found other ways of buying the products they wanted. So the store pushed one incentive after another, organised sales, gave seasonal discounts, advertised constantly. Yet, its management refused to look at internal processes until now. Using a group of college students, the local business school finally did a survey of 'customer care'. In this survey, the students described step-by-step their interactions with the store. The store management was most surprised to find out that their salesmen were constantly interrupted in the middle of their sales pitch to run internal errands. When confronted, the supervisors explained that since support staff had been dramatically reduced, salesmen had to do most of the carry-and-fetch work. What they didn't realise was that interrupted customers would walk away without buying.

ORDER THE OUTPUT FROM YOUR PROCESS

The first step in placing oneself in our customer's shoes is to order the output from our very own processes—incognito if possible. This should give us a better understanding of what to expect in terms of delivery, service and quality than what we read in our statistics. Quite enlightening too. I have done this with several managers responsible for some output or other. They are usually astounded by the response an outsider gets to a request. The difference of vision of the situation from the inside to the outside is quite amazing. Here are three questions to ask ourselves about our customers.

Q. How often do we listen to what they have to say?
Q. Have these customers been satisfied with the service we provide them?
Q. Are these customers' requirements clear to everyone in the team?

TALK TO CUSTOMERS ABOUT WHAT THEY DO WITH YOUR OUTPUT

If you can, follow a customer through their own processes and operations. You will find out how they *use* what you provide and how you can improve it. You can be very surprised by what the customers do with your product. This is particularly relevant for internal customers. Most support functions in companies produce quantities of reports. These reports are supposed to help decision-making. Yet do they? It is actually very difficult to evaluate the usefulness of internal support functions such as Finance or Marketing. Obviously such functions have an important role, or they wouldn't be so *powerful*. Yet, if we get down to cases we will often find that people don't actually use much of the output of these departments. They rely on some specific items, however, totally. How could we try to separate what is *really* being used from the rest?

This problem is accrued, both with internal and external

customers, by the fact that someone, somewhere always uses that extra bit of service or this extra report. Nobody else does, but they do. If you decide to cut it, they will probably resist your decision and complain loudly. This could lead to further problems and so forth. So, why not keep doing the extra bit—by doing so, you can justify a bigger budget next year.

In the trading company of a blue chip corporation, the finance department produces a five-year-plan every year. The odd thing about this five-year plan is that everyone in the company dismisses it as a waste of time and effort. It is often referred to as the annual raindance, a bunch of numbers that nobody looks at. Yet, producing this plan requires about fifteen finance analysts working full time for about two months. Why? Standard answer: because head office wants it. Has anyone checked what head office really wants? Oh, not really, but they are always ringing and asking for more detailed information. So, year in, year out this goes on. What value is it to the company's end customer? Head office probably knows.

THE NEXT PROCESS IS THE CUSTOMER

Quality consultant Masaaki Imai[9] tells the following story about quality guru K Ishikawa.

Ishikawa was investigating some surface scratches found on certain steel sheets. When he suggested to the engineer in charge of that particular process that his team review the problems together with the engineers of the following process, the engineer replied, 'Do you mean to tell us that we should go examine the problems with our enemies?' To this, Ishikawa replied, `You must not think of them as your enemies. You must think of the next process as your customer. You should visit your customer every day to make sure he is satisfied with your product.' However the engineer insisted 'How could I do such a thing? If I show up in their workshop they'll think I've come to spy on them!' This incident gave Ishikawa the inspiration for his now famous phrase: 'The next process is the customer'.

It is important to realise that the customer—whether internal or external—is not simply a person but is also part of a process. The customer has problems because the customer needs to *do* something. To understand what the customer values, we must know more about the processes that drive him or her—the goals, the constraints, the rewards and the punishments that motivate his or her actions.

4

STEP 2: SKETCH THE PROCESS

◇

Once we understand better how our output fits within the customer's own processes and what they are likely to be sensitive to, we can start unravelling our own flow of operations. At this stage we will try to follow the process from *order* to *delivery* to have a better idea of the *sequence of tasks* involved. Of course, the obvious way of mapping this process would be to go and ask everybody to describe what they do. This is quite easy to do, unfortunately the results are not very operational.

Practical Tip: if using interviews as a means of collecting process data, be wary of a number of pitfalls:

1. people tend to tell you what they want you to know;
2. people will also tend to tell you what they think you want to hear;
3. we have a tendency to hear what we expect in what other people tell us.

No one is actually lying, but natural biases can considerably warp the output of interviews.

There is quite a gap between what people say and what they actually do—mostly because they don't remember the sequence of their actions, rather, they will explain the reasons for them. There are several methods to sketch out a process, some involving detailed questionnaires, others based on computer programs. For the sake of simplicity, I favour the walk-through method.

WALK THROUGH THE PROCESS

The idea is childishly simple. Order form in hand, you can follow the process from start to finish. At each stage, you can ask the person concerned to drop what he or she is doing and treat the order you are following. You will be able to get:

- *An operational understanding*: a good idea of the tasks involved in the process and their level of difficulty.
- *Timing*: A feel for the difference between value-added time and waiting time (such as transport, queuing, etc.)
- *Professional opinion*: By listening to the people explain to you what they actually do, you will get an idea of the operational difficulties they face.
- *Morale*: People respond positively to interest in their job. From the manager's point of view, this is a good way to show interest whilst accomplishing a necessary task.

From the walk-through we can sketch out a general outline of the process. It doesn't need to be too precise at this stage, we will work on the task-by-task map later. What this does is give us a good idea of the scope of the process and the main fragmentation points.

Practical Tip: Take particular note when two people have a 'very good' or 'very bad' working relationship. It usually means that they are in constant contact with each other. This makes for a great social life, but it also points to a disconnected process at this particular point. These people talk to each other often because they frequently need to resolve issues.

GATHER ALL FORMS AND DOCUMENTATION

As you walk through the process gather a copy of all the forms and documents that surround it. It will give you an idea of how 'bureaucratised' the process has become, and how standardised it is. Then ask a few questions:

Q: Is this form necessary? Indeed, is this whole part of the process necessary?
Q: Is this form easy to understand and fill in? Can I fill it in without knowing anything about it? How long does it take?

Q: Could I follow these instructions without ever having done it
   beforehand?
Q: Can we design easier-to-use documents?

When redesigning processes at a major oil company, the teams
use a 'brown-walling' approach: they cover the walls of a meeting room with brown paper on which they stick all the documents
related to the process in question. They then order these documents in the sequence of the workflow and use the resulting
'wall' as a basis for redesigning the process. This is quite a
spectacular and fun technique that gives a good idea of what the
organisation thinks the process is. The risk is to miss operations
that people do, which do not appear in the documentation.

GET THE REDESIGN TEAM TOGETHER

As a result of walking through the process, one can get a good idea
of who needs to be involved in the redesign team. Basically, we need
one member from each of the constituent teams. This person should
preferably be the team leader.

1. Redesign activities are part of the managerial role, and it falls
   within the scope of the team leader rather than the individual team
   members.
2. It shows commitment from the team leaders to be willing to
   participate.
3. It helps the overall manager see how his team leaders function *as
   a team*.

If the team leader doesn't know the specifics about the work being
processed by the team, it might be a good idea to invite both the
team leader and the member responsible for the work to the sessions.

This process redesign team is not permanent. It is created *ad hoc*
for the redesign exercise and will only exist as a workgroup for the
five or six days needed for the actual redesign and implementation.
The members of the team are actually part of the working process,
and not staff pulled out to create a special 'process re-engineering'
team which would look at several processes in a row. The *ad hoc*
aspect of the team is very important to avoid several group dynamics
issues.

Practical Tip: Don't limit yourself when picking the members of the team. Don't exclude someone because you feel they are discontented or 'difficult'. The exercise is very task-centred and the group dynamics are likely to remain minimal. Difficult or discontented people can actually be strong drivers in this instance.

DON'T FORGET THE CUSTOMER

Teams often 'forget' the person who might have the most to bring to the process: the customer. There are several valid reasons for this:

- *We are not necessarily close to the customers*: although we know each other fairly well, the customer is usually part of the 'out-group' and not someone we feel comfortable to include in our discussions.
- *It might be embarrassing*: remember that we might not actually want the customer to know how we operate—they might use it against us at a future date.
- *They might not be interested*: customers usually think they have other things to do than spend time with their suppliers; 'I expect my delivery team to deliver' is a common attitude.

WE KNOW WHO THE CLIENT IS, BUT WHO IS THE CUSTOMER?

Dealing with the 'customer' can sometimes be awkward, particularly at corporate level because our client is not necessarily our customer. In most cases, our point of contact is someone from the client firm's purchasing department. This person has their own ideas about what they want from us, but so do their CEO, their accountants, and our true customer. It can be an operator on a machine, or the person who schedules work in the plant. It is sometimes very confusing since each of these relevant individuals will probably have conflicting views of what they actually expect from us. In this particular context, we will consider our customer to be the one who actually *uses* our output in his or her work. This person is not always easy to talk to, considering the normal communication channels from firm to firm, but the effort is usually worth it.

5

STEP 3: PROCESS MAPPING

❖

Once you have a fairly good idea of the general outline of the process and you have put together your process redesign team, it is time to run a process mapping session. Operational process mapping works on the following principle: each operation will be represented by a post-it note. The process is then represented by physical parts that can be reorganised differently. Representing operations by physical one-step stickers helps the team to manipulate concepts as if they were objects. In this way they get down to re-organising the order of the tasks on a practical basis. The written—as opposed to spoken—medium also helps to limit verbal game-playing and focuses the work of the team on technical and professional problems rather than on leadership and influence issues.

AGENDA

At the heart of the process redesign programme is a two-day intensive work session. Once the process has been outlined by walking through it and talking to its customers, we are ready to go ahead and redesign. This is best done by taking two solid days away from routine work and focusing on this particular process. Here is what the agenda for the two days can look like:

Day 1	9:30	Welcome and presentation
	10:00	Warm-up: team talk
	10:15	Process mapping
	12:00	Process map
	13:30	Process issues
	14:00	Classical solutions
	14:30	Warm-up: team talk
	14:45	Customer vision
	15:00	Process redesign
	17:00	Presentation of new process
Day 2	9:30	Welcome and presentation

10:00	Warm-up: team talk
10:15	Process weak points
11:00	Barriers to implementation
12:00	Influence diagram
13:30	Conditions for success
14:00	Warm-up: team talk
14:15	Action list
15:00	Actions presentation
15:45	Action grouping
16:00	Action distribution
17:00	Wrap-up

START WITH A WARM-UP

How can members of a process team talk to each other without getting waylaid by reluctance, power games or plain distraction? Whenever we deal with any collective process, we must take into consideration two different levels of interaction: the task level and the social level. 'Task' is about getting things done. 'Social' is about dealing with the other members of the group (alliances, pecking order, support, teasing, competition and all those fun things).

If a group is left to itself, we can observe how it naturally responds to these two fundamental tensions, oscillating from one type of interaction to the other.

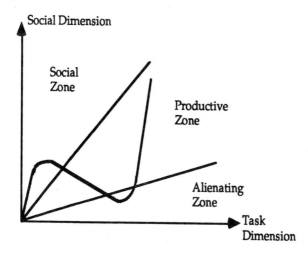

To get the team—people who usually know each other but haven't necessarily worked with each other before—started as fast as possible, we can warm up with a 'team talk' session. Team talk is actually different from conversation. Conversation is what we naturally do when we talk to one another: we express verbally what goes through our minds. It's usually not particularly ordered, and most of the fun comes out of arguing a point or kidding each other. The aim of team talk is to convey information to the group without getting entangled in the social dimension. Team talk is not used all the time but only at specific moments when things have to get cleared up before 'normal' conversation can resume.

The rules of team talk are that:

1. Everybody speaks in turn.
2. People state what they want to say without expecting any immediate reaction from the others.
3. Others listen and do not reply.
4. Conversation starts only when everyone has had their say.

Because it is actually quite difficult to disconnect the 'social' dimension that makes us want to answer, or intervene when somebody is speaking (usually to tell them that they're wrong, or that things have changed, or any other comment), the team talk technique will help to focus the process team as a warm-up. The idea is to follow the Indian Pow Wow procedure and actually let each and every one have their say before any discussion takes place.

This idea of separating the task dimension from the social dimension will run throughout the techniques we use to make process redesign a success. In these two days of mapping, redesigning, and preparing the implementation, the team will hardly have the time to go through the usual 'team formation' cycle. In general, teams go through the following phases:

1. *Forming*: Individuals come together, talk about the aims of the group, its title, membership, how it will relate to the rest of the organisation. Individuals seek to make their mark, test each other out, establish their status, power, etc.
2. *Storming*: A conflict period in which aims, individual roles and power, work methods, etc. are in dispute. Earlier assumptions are challenged. Personal hostilities come out into the open.
3. *Norming*: The group establishes rules and practices about how it

takes decisions, what behaviour is acceptable, how open people are with each other, etc.

4. *Performing*: The group has now resolved these issues and can focus on *getting the job done*, with less attention to its own processes, structure, etc.

Since we haven't got the time to let the team go through its normal development, we need to compensate by relying heavily on the structure of the exercise we put the team through to produce the desired outputs. In this sense, the sessions will be very output driven. At the end of day two we should have produced:

- A process workflow map.
- A redesigned map.
- An action plan.
- Individual action sheets.

The techniques proposed may sometimes seem a bit heavy handed, or bureaucratic. They are actually *designed* to keep the group focused on solving problems rather than on *interacting* with each other. The post-it notes in particular guarantee that each member's voice is heard equally and cannot be suppressed through an act of authority or misplaced leadership. Maintaining the integrity of individual post-its is quite important because it is a symbol of the integrity of the process itself. Furthermore, the task level of specificity of the post-its ensures that discussions happen at a sufficiently detailed level to engage professional—as opposed to territorial—exchanges. This doesn't mean that no social interaction is allowed, on the contrary, but simply that the framework works as a team integrator for very short term, *ad hoc* team formations.

DRAWING OUT THE TASKS

Once the group is focused, we will ask each participant to write down on a post-it note every individual operation he or she does as part of the process. For the process redesign to be operational we need to get down to task level. At the end of the day this is where practical changes will need to be made. The closer we are to actual task level, the easier it will be to implement the new process simply because people will go out of the room knowing precisely what to do. Furthermore, being specific about tasks gives the other participants a good look at what their colleagues actually do. What appears to be a side-benefit can turn out later to be of the utmost importance since staff can see how resolving their own problems in practice often creates problems upstream.

The market analysis department of a large British company used to produce bi-monthly reports for front-line managers giving them their market position as regards their competitors. This report took about one week to compile and format, and was usually done just before it went out. However, the department asked for constant data updates from IT on a 'just-in-case basis'. The idea was that if the data arrived early, they could start early with the analysis. Starting early also meant revising data as time went on. So, usually, the analysis was left till the end of the period.

It was only through mapping the entire process that the department realised how much work they actually gave to IT with their update requests—work they didn't even use afterwards! IT and market analysis then opted for one data transfer one week before the report was produced. The data would then be 'closed', ie not updated further till the following transfer. The end customers—the front-line managers—were astonished by the work required to produce a report that only received a cursory glance, in order to check for 'outrageous' changes in market position. As one manager put it, 'I trust my own reps far more than any data-crunching "they" give me'.

EVERY OPERATION IS REPRESENTED BY A POST-IT NOTE

This enables us to visualise the operations and place them in a *flow*. Each operation becomes a physical object which can be moved around on the board. The post-its are written according to the *post-it rules*:

The post-it rules are:

1. Write in large capital letters.
2. One idea or fact per note.
3. Write *full* sentences (subject, verb, complement) rather than topics.

4. Paye no atention to sppelling!
5. Be specific: keep to facts rather than opinions.

With operations represented by post-it notes, the flow can be recon-structed *bottom-up*, from physical evidence—rather than opinion. Operations need to fit with each other for the reconstruction to be valid!

EACH POST-IT IS CHECKED FOR COMPREHENSION

Each post-it is read to the group to check understanding. In this way, every participant gets a good sense of what happens in the other functional units. This is probably the most 'heavy-going' part of the workshop, yet it is absolutely essential.

1. The facilitator draws a circle at the centre of the board.
2. When participants have finished writing their post-it notes, they stick them up on the board regardless of order on the left-hand side of the circle.
3. When all post-its are on the board, the facilitator takes them one by one, regardless of order. He or she reads them out loud to the team and checks for comprehension—not agreement.
4. If one post-it is not understood by someone in the team, the facilitator asks the originator to explain what they meant.
5. If the phrasing of the post-it needs changing, the team can help the originator in coming up with a new satisfying phrasing. How-ever, the facilitator does not modify the original post-it. He or she gives it back to the originator who will then write a new one. It is very important to maintain the integrity of everyone's post-its. For instance, even if a post-it seems irrelevant it should not be thrown away—it can be 'parked' at the most.

FACILITATOR RULES

The facilitator can be anyone in the group. It is best if he or she is not the team leader, and if the role rotates. The facilitator's role is mainly to:

■ Make sure everyone understands what is stated on the cards or on the board.

- Occasionally refocus the group if the social dimension takes over for too long.
- In discussions, ask questions that will balance out the gist of the group's thinking: if the group is being negative about an idea, ask for the positive sides—and vice-versa.

The facilitator doesn't have much impact on the actual content of the team's thinking. He or she may intervene if they have something to contribute, but as team member, not as a facilitator. Furthermore, the facilitator cannot modify anything written on a card or anything expressed by anyone. If an idea is unclear to a member of the group, the facilitator can ask the originator to rephrase it. When working with cards or post-its the facilitator *never* modifies someone else's card. If the card is unclear, the facilitator can give it back to the person who will then write a new card. The use of a facilitator is to give a focus to the group. In doing so, we can easily limit the competitive or argumentative dimension of the social interaction. It is good practice to take turns to be the facilitator so that the task doesn't become linked to one specific member of the team.

THE POST-ITS ARE PLACED ON A BOARD IN SEQUENCE

The process flow is reconstructed from the experience of the participants. In practice, the facilitator will follow the instructions given

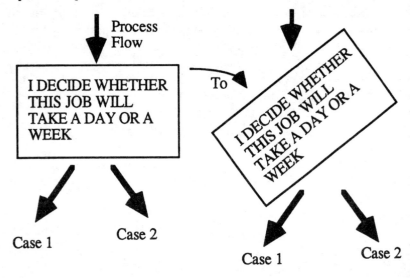

by the relevant participants. He or she needs to keep an eye out for branching points in processes where different cases will be separated and follow different routes. To be rigorous, these branching points can be highlighted by turning the post-it at a 45° angle.

The workflows will appear from placing the post-its sequentially on the board. As the session progresses, the entire process should appear *at an operational level*.

Practical Tip: start from the end point rather than the start point. By doing so you can reconstruct the necessary order of the operations, and are less likely to let one slip by.

INPUTS AND OUTPUTS

Blue (or any colour other than red) post-its are used to represent input and output points to the process (information/service/product) from outside the process. These points are particularly important because they tend to hide strong dependencies. As they are not in our immediate control, we can easily ignore them, a classic case of 'someone else's turf'. Yet these interfaces may bring their own problems and delays. It is very important to be able to highlight where the processes connect.

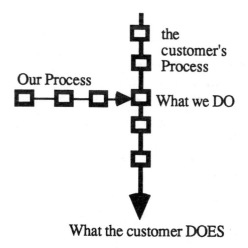

THE CUSTOMER PROCESS IS SKETCHED OUT VERTICALLY

In particular, we can detail the customer's process. We can then place our own output in the customer's process and see how our actions help or hinder theirs.

This is why the customer's presence is so important. By detailing their process, and understanding what they do with our output, we get a better idea of what they actually need. This will serve as a strong guiding principle at the redesign stage. As we modify the structure of the workflows, we will have to make a number of changes which might have an impact on the customer. Understanding the customer's process helps to make decisions and trade-offs.

DRAW IN CURRENT FEEDBACK LOOPS

Where and how do checks happen? What are the most current rework paths? Feedback loops are usually the most time-consuming part of any process. They can double the delivery time for a minute rework. Nevertheless they're usually happily ignored by all who work in the process, neatly filed under the 'we've got a problem again' heading. Some such 'problems' happen often enough to be considered to be a routine part of the process, albeit unwanted. Drawing these feed-back loops in the flows can focus our thinking at the redesign phase.

In redesigning the market analysis report process already mentioned, the team found out that much heavy number-crunching was done before the data were checked. This involved a number of 12 to 24 hour program runs, when the machines were available. In effect, if some data inconsistency was spotted at the analysis stage, the whole thing had to be run again—adding from one to two weeks more to the overall process. By inserting early data inconsistency checks, the overall lead-time and workload of the process was dramatically reduced.

USE RED POST-ITS TO FLAG PROBLEM PLACES

Where the usual snags happen, we place a red flag. These snags are supposed to disappear in the redesigned process! They represent standard problems which keep cropping up. In most cases, people have been moaning about these problems for years, but because of their rather diffuse nature it was always difficult to do anything about them. By flagging them at the mapping stage, we make sure we deal with these annoying glitches as we redesign the process.

MEASURING EFFICIENCY BY THE LEAD-TIME

It is always very difficult to measure productivity in functional processes. This is a particularly acute issue as we walk away from production and deal with administrative or managerial processes. Overall, the best indicator of value production is *time*. Time to delivery, as well as the proportion of time spent on each operation. The time it takes to do an operation from beginning to end is a clear indicator of how buttoned down the process is. Furthermore, time is usually linked to how many cases one can actually treat—there are only so many hours in the day!

Many people get confused around the productivity issue. At the end of the day, productivity can be defined by the simple ratio of output/time. For most people, productivity can be increased in only two ways: either you throw more resources at the process, or you get people to work faster. The assumption here is that the number of cases dealt with is directly linked to each work station's productivity.

If one person processes three jobs per day, close to the end of the day, the schedule will look like this:

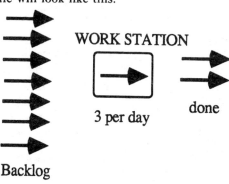

WORK STATION

3 per day

done

Backlog

So, if we want to increase productivity, we need to either get this person to process more jobs per day:

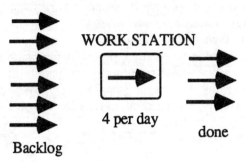

Which usually means working harder, or we could get a second person to help, at the original rhythm:

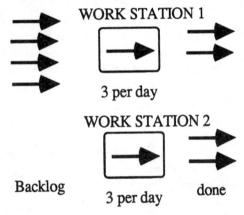

The assumption is that all other quantities are set. However, what we label as 'workstation' is in fact a process: a series of sequential operations. We tend to dismiss the productivity gains which can be obtained from redesigning this process. If the lead-time of the operation is halved by simply reorganising the tasks, then one person will be twice as efficient—without working any harder, but simply by doing less stupid things. Just think about it, how much time do you spend looking for the right file or right information whenever you start a new task? All this time spent at non-value added work is waiting time for the jobs in the backlog.

WORKING SMARTER, NOT WORKING HARDER

Time is a good indicator because it is spent equally, whether one's activity is value-adding or totally useless. This happens because many useless tasks are actually inscribed *in* the process. We all agree that spending half an hour locating the right person to talk to in the organisation for a simple request is a total waste of time from the point of view of the output (irritating too), yet, in the current organisation of things we need to do this in order to talk to that person. In effect we have worked hard for half an hour at not doing the next step! And the worse thing about it is that we cannot bypass it!

> In a French factory where one production line was redesigned, the operators had two diverging views of the redesign work. The operators from the other lines were strongly opposed to redesign work because they felt that since the redesign effort, the new line's operators 'worked like crazy'. In contrast, the operators on the redesigned line were very favourable to redesign because they felt that they did not 'waste as much time as before'. What happened was that in the redesign action much wasteful work had been cut out, such as moving about the plant looking for the right tools, going to the other side of the building to fetch a trolley to carry heavy containers to and from the line, and so forth. These tasks were actually felt to be a burden by the operators and in the redesign workshop they suggested that something be done about it. In the new system they didn't spend quite as much time away from their work on annoying, interrupting and physically trying tasks. However, in the old system they would often pause for a chat with operators on other lines as they lugged things around. Not seeing them come around anymore, the other operators concluded that they now 'worked like crazy'.

TIME THE OPERATIONS

On the board, under each operation, write two time values:

1. The time it actually takes to *do* the work.
2. The time the work stays at this stage of the process (ie the difference between in-time and out-time).

To be rigorous one needs to conduct a time-measurement study at this stage to know precisely how much time is spent at each station. In practice, such level of precision is often unnecessary. People have a very good idea of how long it takes them to do something and how long the job stays on their desk. The overall time spent at a station can be easily correlated because the other people in the process (before and after stages) usually know exactly when they've sent work out, and when they get work in. So, altogether, the time picture we draw is fairly accurate—certainly accurate enough for our purpose.

Practical Tip: if, as a facilitator, you see that someone is hesitant about timing, ask him or her to remember a specific instance of doing the job—like 'the last time you did this'. Remembering usually triggers more remembering and helps to anchor the thought process.

RELATIVE TIME

As we look at the process we can wonder at the relative efficiency of the tasks processed. We can ask ourselves a few key questions about the time we spend doing things:

Q. Are the longest tasks the most value adding?
Q. Do we spend a long time on some things that only add marginal value to the ultimate output?
Q. What does the customer think?

6

STEP 4: REDESIGNING THE PROCESS

◇

Once the process map is drawn out, it is time to actually redesign. In practice, this means we are going to change the flow of operations from input to output. In many cases we will end up changing operations themselves, but to start with we simply want to re-order them! But first:

DON'T PANIC

At this stage, there usually is a rather awkward moment. We have finished mapping the entire process and we think 'Gosh, it's a mess!' We know that we are going to have to simplify it, but all that detailed information can look rather daunting. Take a break, and let it sink in.

HALVE THE LEAD-TIME

The strategy is simple: we are going to ask the team to make the entire process fit *within one day*. Of course, we realise that, most of the time, this is far from realistic. In practice, we expect to halve the lead-time. But this improbable goal helps to focus the team spirit on *what to do next*. The team will usually scream blue murder, or at the very least grumble about impossibilities and outrageous demands. Fine—let them! The team has already been working very hard and is suddenly faced with an apparently impossible task. We can expect some frustration and it is good to let off steam.

The sense of challenge which sets in is key to the success of the redesign. Yes, it looks impossible. Yes, we have done it before. Yes, we can do this—or are you telling me that you are not as good as your other colleagues? What needs to stand out at this critical point is that the challenge is a technical one, not an attitudinal one. The people in the room are competent professionals and we want to reinforce the *working smarter* aspect of redesign. Forget about commitment, about giving more to the company and so on. The redesign exercise is set as a *technical puzzle*, meant to valorise professional expertise. This professional angle will get things started on a low-key, hard-work basis and, as such, deal with many unwanted potential group dynamics. The moment the team sees it as a technical challenge, the participants are quite likely to have a serious go at it—and even enjoy doing so.

Practical Tip: in the letting off steam phase, pay particular attention to people's objections. They usually are symptoms of very real problems—even though the 'impossible' conclusion is most likely wrong. Those objections can be used later as a way to focus the team on technical difficulties that need to be overcome.

ZERO INVESTMENT

The second rule for process redesign is *no further investment*. As T Ohno used to say, 'use your ideas, not your money.' By giving the team a goal and a constraint—process in one day and zero investment—you actually set up a creative tension which will help to direct the team's activity towards *feasible* redesign. Zero investment is a particularly useful rule to get the team out of the 'more resources needed' sloppy thinking. Clearly, since they are the people working on the process, they will not want to increase their workload. If they cannot crack the productivity question by the standard answer (more of the same), they will progressively look at the re-organisation-of-tasks angle as a way out.

Zero investment need not be respected to the letter at the end of the day. Some minor investment here and there will probably be needed; as the saying goes, 'There's no such thing as a free lunch'. Yet these investments will likely be small and delocalised. Without the zero investment rule, teams tend to dream up the 'magical gimmick solution':

- The super-duper computer that will do it all.
- The wizard expert who will know it all.

■ The nice, cheap, reliable contractor who will do the work for you, and take you out to lunch too.

■ Doubling the department's budget so you can hire more staff,

This is work, and this is the real world. Teams need to be reminded that *they* will have to implement what they come up with *tomorrow*—and that they won't get any additional budget to do so. Particularly so when one considers how difficult it is to obtain budgets for cross-functional work. In the end, this creates a strong incentive to come up with clever ideas.

PROCESS HANG-UPS

In order to redesign processes, we must understand a few typical process issues that appear time and time again. Processes reflect the thinking behind the organising principles. Fragmentation and specialisation are very efficient for control and exactitude but from an overall process point of view they are terribly inefficient. However, we are now so accustomed to the way work is organised that it can be hard to see otherwise. As we shall see later, 'processes' are quite predictable. There is no magical managerial quality to processes, and no need for glamorous expensive consultants to get them right. A process is nothing more than a sequence of dependent actions, and can be studied in the same way as any other regular phenomenon. Process issues are not even very complex, they have simply been overlooked for so long that we can easily find some *major* things wrong with them without having to be rocket scientists.

Too many hand-offs

How many hand-offs occur from start to finish? Often, the tasks themselves do not take long to do, but the hand-offs from one person to the other can be lengthy. First, these hand-offs seldom happen one item at a time but in batch form. In addition, operations take varying amounts of time and this will create stockpiles and bottle-necks at several points throughout the process.

These many hand-offs—sometimes up to 9 or 12—also make any improvement difficult. Even if we squeeze more productivity out of the value-adding parts, we still retain the overall inefficiency. Such a structure is also unlikely to be customer focused because each individual specialist is separated from the customers by all the other links. It can also make for frustrating and meaningless work, as people will work on disjointed, fragmented and repetitious tasks without any overall understanding of their purpose. Having a vision of the entire product has been shown to be a strong motivational element for many people. Without the vision such a structure will deprive most organisations of this added motivational source.

No one is in charge

Similarly, we find that no one is in charge of the process. In fact hardly anyone is even aware of entire processes. Most people's reference is their department: their supervisor, their colleagues and their subordinates. As such, this encourages overall dysfunctional behaviour where the next step becomes 'the enemy'. There is no enemy, there is no 'out there', we're all in the same boat. Yet in many organisations functional rivalries are still more important than servicing the customers. Most people respect a leader, not an idea.

Obsolete assumptions

When they restrict themselves to the traditional framework, people often accept obsolete assumptions. 'We cannot give information to our customer because they will use it against us in negotiations.' 'No one can replace a specialist, particularly not one of those "expert systems".' 'Marketing and engineering have mutually incompatible missions' and so forth. In many companies some fundamentally accepted tenets are sometimes surprising to the outsider. Yet, for the people in these companies, such statements are accepted as true, and they are often bewildered when told that other firms successfully do without them.

Too many checks and controls

A classical fragmented and specialised organisation of work is also likely to generate too many checks and controls. These checks and controls were originally created to fight the problems of fragmenting tasks, but as time goes by, they become part of the problem themselves. Too many checks and controls involve inevitable delays, and shift the emphasis away from quality. They go against process ownership and reinforce fragmentation. More than anything, they stifle any innovation or creativity because they were purposefully built to avoid anything 'not done by the book'.

Automating a mess!

Finally, IT has often been used as a panacea. In many cases, people have automated the existing process and sometimes gained a little productivity from it. However, if the underlying organisational issues are not resolved first, all we get is an automated mess. This usually requires heavy maintenance and support and does not significantly improve processes. IT needs to be seen as an enabling tool. Modern databases and networks enable us to do things no one could do before. Anyone who needs it can now have access to information. Furthermore, IT enables us to build 'expert systems' that capture the expert knowledge of individuals and can be a great support tool for managers. The aim is not to replace people with machines, but to replace specialists with generalists. An expert system enables a generalist to do the work of a specialist without having the same limitations. IT should not be seen as a way to automate what we already do, but as a powerful tool to rethink many of our assumptions about 'what can be done'.

ONE THING AT A TIME

It actually makes a lot of sense to condense the process lead-time. Ultimately, it will force us to process operations sequentially. This means that our productivity shoots up because most errors in processing, and most lost time, come from putting down the task to do something else and starting it again later. This is obvious on a personal level, and crucial at the organisational level.

Unfortunately, most organisational processes are interconnected with many other routine tasks which need to happen all the time. As a result, work is constantly interrupted. The first lesson in organisational efficiency is to try to re-create some process integrity: I start and I finish in the same block of time. This might not be practical—but it is the only way to ensure that operations are tightened up.

BE READY FOR THE IMPROVEMENT KILLERS

It is usually at this point that most people's anguishes will become apparent. The natural reaction to change tends to be 'we can't do that', for whatever reason. It is important to insist that *it is an exercise*. Nobody is expected to actually go out and do it tomorrow. We just want to know whether it is possible to get the process down to one day. One of the reasons that improvement can be so difficult is that some people are dedicated improvement killers. Know thine enemy! Actually, it is *by their sign* that you know them; here are a few classics:

It's not possible

To some people, anything that is not already done, is simply not possible. Impossible to convince, these people can really bring a team down, particularly when the team is experimenting with wild ideas. The trouble is that most of their objections seem to be valid!

It's not our job

Worse than the 'it's not possible' type, these people actually refuse to deal with any issue that doesn't fall within the narrowly defined parameters of what they consider to be 'their job'. Organisational problems never appear in job descriptions, so they often have good cause to feel that 'this is not part of their job'. The annoying thing is that they make anybody who does want to put in extra time for the company feel like idiots.

It shouldn't be like this

The most resilient type. These people cannot accept that things are not as they should be. By constantly referring to how things are supposed to be, they avoid dealing with the practicalities of real life. Their impact on the group is to magically turn any problem-solving session into a good ol' whinge session—out of which everybody comes out feeling self-righteous, frustrated or downright depressed. There is nothing much to do with these guys except suggest they go into politics!

The answer is obvious

The 'answer is obvious' types tend to be very clever, quick, think-on-your-feet people. They always argue for the rightness of a solution without taking into consideration other people's reactions. They don't think that they might just have a real problem about it—but that they aren't ready to talk about it just yet. Not a bad sort really, but they can grate on everybody's nerves—particularly top management fat cats.

I'm already doing it

Often a variation of 'the answer is obvious'. Particularly defensive people will try to argue that they are 'already doing it' even when that is blatantly not true. Difficult to get around, because showing them they are wrong means major loss of face, and letting it go means covering-up. The best solution is probably to let peer pressure work on them.

I'll do it tomorrow

Your usual procrastinator; agrees to everything and never does anything. Stop talking to them and find a by-pass.

MAKE IT POSSIBLE

Once the exercise has been accepted by the team, the issue of trade-offs will appear. Many people will say, 'Sure, I can do this, but it means that these other super-important things won't get done'. Fine. They are usually right about that too. The answer is that we have decided to tackle this particular process, so, rightly or wrongly, it gets priority. If other tasks need to be shelved, ok—for now. In practice, there is no need to worry, people usually find a way to do both in the end. Most of the reactions one gets at this stage come more from anticipation of over-commitment than any rational evaluation.

Stress that very few things are actually impossible. Costly, maybe. Impractical, certainly. But a solution is a solution, no matter how costly or impractical. It is usually all we need to get the discussion started on how, to actually make it work within the zero investment constraint. Having a place to start from makes it a lot easier to be creative collectively.

Practical Tip: if someone is really defensive and keeps saying 'it's impossible', ask this person to state three ways of making it happen—no matter how impractical—before giving the reasons why it is impossible.

HOW DO WE DO IT?

If we are dealing with specific process issues, some of the structures created by the organisation of work can be changed by using a few tested principles. These principles can be applied in a variety of situations and can serve as guiding concepts to rebuild our organisations along processes rather than functions. These are indeed recipes, and have to be handled as such. Don't be dogmatic. At the end of the day, we want to design something that works better than what we have today. The emphasis is on *work*. Some people familiar with process work might want to go to the extreme textbook solution right away. For one thing, text books aren't always right, and for another, extreme solutions are not necessarily realistic to implement. The following principles should be regarded as general guidelines, not absolute rules.

DON'T AUTOMATE: ELIMINATE

Michael Hammer's slogan is more than relevant. Be radical in redesigning processes—start by the question: 'Do we really need this?' Flexibility in a department is linked to its capacity to move from old to new processes in order to accommodate changing customer needs. In order to foster this we need to establish *a kill-date for each new process in place*. Organisations end up in a mess because of the sedimentation of years of obsolete old processes never being disconnected.

THINK PARALLEL

For convenience, or through the force of habit, we deal sequentially with tasks which are not necessarily dependent. Although A does not have to be completed before B starts, we usually do B after A. This sequential dependency makes the process far longer than it needs to be. You can end up waiting for someone's answer before starting the next step—although you could start right away. If there is a single greatest source of improvement in most processes it is to place non-dependent tasks in parallel!

Just as when cooking a dish, all the ingredients do not necessarily need to have been prepared before starting the cooking, although some people actually prefer to do so. They can also prefer to have the dish cooked before they lay the table:

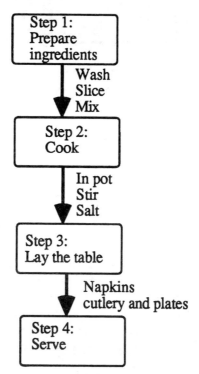

In some cases it actually makes good sense to do these various operations in parallel: I can start cooking some ingredients before they have all been prepared. I can lay the table while the food is cooking. Serving, however, is truly dependent. I can't serve unless I have prepared the ingredients, cooked, and laid the table.

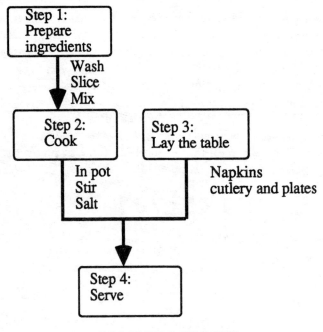

SPLIT PROCESSES

Another fundamental principle of the traditional organisation of work is the notion that a process must fit all cases. Consequently, processes have built in a great number of alternative routes and contingencies to be able to deal with both the simplest and the most complex cases. Some processes have been worked out in such thorough details that the very procedure fills entire books, with pages and pages of contingencies that try to predict every possible case. Of course, these books are seldom read and often unreadable. However, this assumption creates numerous problems. For one thing, if a number of 'simple' cases lie in the queue after a 'complex' case, they will suffer the delays that occur in processing the complex case.

For instance, suppose that you are waiting in the queue at a railway station. You want a straightforward London-Manchester ticket, return, second class, no frills. Your train leaves in ten minutes. Three ticket tills are open and there is a queue of about five persons at each. You are almost there, with only one person in front of you. Unfortunately, the woman in front of you is trying to get a refund for the Aberdeen-Glasgow-London ticket her husband bought a month ago and never used because he got a lift with a friend. Watch those minutes go by!

TILL 1	TILL 2	TILL 3	Probable Job Time
◯	◯	◯	
◯	◯	◯	20 mns
◯	◯	◯	3 mns
◯	◯◯	◯	3 mns
◯	◯	◯	10 mns
		◯	3 mns

As you sweat it out, and restlessly consider changing queues wondering whether the four people to your left would have time to pass before the woman is done, you also start cursing the railway and all it entails. The truth of the matter is that from the railway's point of view, it doesn't matter who comes first. Their problem is to deal with each customer in turn:

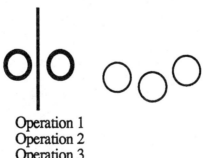

Operation 1
Operation 2
Operation 3
Any special requests ?
Operation 4
Operation 5
Thank you very much,
Have a nice trip!

Your problem, however, is very different: you want to get from London to Manchester with the least aggravation:

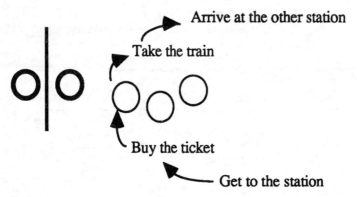

Arrive at the other station

Take the train

Buy the ticket

Get to the station

So the order in which tickets are sold makes a huge difference to your own process. Of course, intelligent railway stations will create a special queue for complex operations.

> The Australian Advance Bank has simplified its process both for its customers and own staff. Forms are no longer required on personal accounts for withdrawals, cash deposits or transfers. As you walk to the counter, the clerk inputs your information in his or her computer terminal and then prints out a small form with all the information. This form divides in two parts: one that you sign and keep for your personal records, and one which stays with the bank for their own records. By this very simple improvement, the bank cuts down considerably on the time and the hassle of making a standard transaction (finding the form, writing it—what's my account number again?) for their clients, and gets rid of the data entry step from the bank's point of view.

Pareto's law is at work on this case:

If we go to the trouble of counting cases in terms of their complexity we tend to find that (1) 80 per cent of the cases processed are perfectly standard and straightforward; (2) about 18 per cent of the cases present a significant difficulty; and (3) only 2 per cent of cases are really complex enough to warrant a high degree of expertise.

These results can then point us towards a different solution. Rather than build one process capable of handling all cases, we can build three separate routes:

- A first one that can be almost entirely automated and which will treat all the standard cases.
- A second route to deal with the more difficult cases. This can usually be handled by a generalist assisted either by an expert system, or a team of expert advice.
- A third route where a specialist will deal exclusively with the most complex cases that no one else can solve.

What we then need is to engineer a filtering point at the entry of the process that will sort cases. Failing that, when one case does not fit into the 'standard' system, it can be diverted to the more complex route. The great advantage of the system is that you can process rapidly the great bulk of demands, and that customers with special requirements will expect to wait a bit longer.

WORK WHERE IT MAKES MOST SENSE, IN THE ORDER THAT MAKES MOST SENSE

In traditional organisations work is organised around specialists, not around where it originates. If the Legal department needs special legal paper pads it won't order them itself. Its job is litigation, not purchasing. It will order new pads from the purchasing department, who will then find vendors, negotiate prices, place orders and pay the invoice. If Purchasing doesn't think special legal pads are worth the extra expense, they are likely to send back normal paper pads to the intense frustration of the lawyers in the Legal department. In many cases the marginal benefits derived (if any) from Purchasing's negotiations are lost in overhead, administrative costs and complexity. From a process point of view, it makes much more sense to do the work where it originates: let the Legal department purchase its pads directly. To quote M. Hammer and J. Champy:[8]

One company we know ran a controlled experiment and learned that it expended $100 in internal cost to buy $3 worth of batteries. It also discovered that 35 per cent of its purchase orders were for amounts of less than $500.

The notion of spending $100 internally to expend $500 or less did not sit well, so the company decided to off-load responsibility for purchasing goods onto the process customers . . . They know from whom to buy and what to pay, because purchasing has negotiated these prices and given the accountants [or other departments] a list of approved vendors. Each operating unit has a credit card with a $500 credit limit.

CASE WORKER OR CASE TEAM

Putting someone in charge of a process can usually solve both the problem of hand-offs and responsibility. The idea is to integrate several jobs into one. One person or team will follow the process from start to finish. The case worker, or case team, can handle the different tasks of the process—with the help of an expert system if necessary. It is not always possible to compress all the steps into one integrated job—sometimes processes spread over several locations. We can then instigate a team of people who will be personally responsible for the hand-off from one location to the next. The overall idea is to re-establish the integrity of the process rather than gather like-tasks together in departments or functions.

Another advantage of using a case worker, or team, is that these persons will own the case they are working on. The case worker provides a single point of contact if anyone wants to know what is going on with application so and so. The case worker is someone the customer can talk to and is able to answer the customer's questions and solve the customer's problems. This can help both with the flexibility, and the service the firm provides to its customers. There are numerous complex issues linked to this point, as in 'Should we create a matrix structure?'. Unfortunately, there are no easy options—solutions have to be worked out locally.

As Womack, Jones and Roos[5] pointed out, one of the main problems with the case worker solution is to ensure a clear career path for this individual. If the individual loses out, first no one will want to take the job, and secondly the job will lose its power and therewith its usefulness. These authors suggest that the function should have a 'university' role, from which the worker is delegated to run processes for a while, and then returns for career advancement and resourcing.

USE TECHNOLOGY AS AN ENABLER

In many cases, technology plays a key role. Yet, that role is not to automate existing procedures, but to enable us to perform tasks we didn't know could be done. Our instinctive tendency when confronted with new technology its to try to make it reproduce what we had before (remember that the first cars were called horseless carriages). Yet, as we master it, we start to open a multitude of applications that no one had originally thought of. After all, Edison invented his recording machine as a device to record one's last words. The true role of technology is to liberate us from constraints that we take for granted.

> For instance, technology enables Pizza Hut in Houston to recall what customers who phone in their orders ordered last time, and if they order the same pizza, to suggest a different kind. If the person agrees, the clerk can then mail them discount coupons with offers customised to that person's taste. In a similar vein, when a customer calls Whirlpool's service line, the call is automatically routed to the service representative that handled that customer's previous call—thus creating a sense of continuity of service in an organisation of more than 800 members.[8]

WARNING: SOLVING YOUR PROBLEMS MAY CREATE THEM FOR OTHERS

The only thing really to worry about when redesigning processes is not to simply shift the problem to someone else. To some extent, this always happens. As processes are modified, everyone who works around this process is going to be affected. Sometimes we will ask our suppliers to provide something or other in a different format. Or our customers will have to accept that some service or other will change. Most of the time, other people will be happy to comply. If they don't, however, they might have very valid reasons.

The question is again about *value-added.* Those who add the most value to the customer should always get priority. In a way, most of our organisations get their priorities wrong when they pamper top executives, and generally treat hands-on workers without much care. Management does not *do* anything. Yes, it is supposed to direct and organise and so on, but at the end of the day it does not directly add much value to the product or service. Some functions such as Finance or IT are actually often quite remote from value to the customer. Yet, because these functions, and Finance in particular, have such great control power, they tend to get things done their way. Power is a reality. Yet power doesn't make customers happy. Power does not make people buy our product. So, when we redesign our processes we must be wary about who we give priority to. Finance has power, certainly, but finance does not do anything the customer would be happy to pay for—nor does Marketing (are you happy to pay for people to *sell* you their product better, or to make sure the *budgets* are respected?). As a rule, to establish priorities keep thinking: *Would our customer be happy to pay for this?*

In a large British electricity company, a senior manager recently discovered that one needed seven signatures for any outside purchase. How had this ever come to happen? A few years ago, a bright young lady with a thieving disposition was working as a temp with the company. She promptly set up a false client address in the computer and paid herself several thousand pounds through the company's purchasing system. She was not bright enough not to be caught, and eventually the whole mess was sorted out.

Not, however, to the satisfaction of the external auditors. This little caper had created an auditing nightmare and there was much work involved to set the books right. The auditors, quite rightly, decided that such a thing should not happen again. Consequently, they set up a policy which required seven managerial authorisations for any outside purchase. No one would be able to take advantage of the system again. Unfortunately, this created such an administrative headache for operational people that suddenly anybody who needed to get things done started to fiddle with the system—which ended up even less controllable than before.

CONCLUSION

To summarise, a well redesigned process should show:

1. 50 per cent lead-time reduction.
2. Parallel processing where possible.
3. Split streams according to complexity.
4. Fewer feed-back loops.
5. No unnecessary steps.

STEP 5: WALK THROUGH, TALK THROUGH

◇

Remember Murphy's Law: whatever can possibly go wrong will probably go wrong. And does this apply to implementation! In fact, it is quite reasonable to expect the implementation of a new process to go wrong. There is no way we could ever think of all the possible contingencies and issues. Nevertheless, forewarned is forearmed. Before we actually go out and do it, we will take the time to figure out what could go wrong and what to do about it. The idea is to be able to:

1. Spot problems early: as soon as they appear
2. Anticipate problems in order to have some elements of a solution ready.

These simple things can make a tremendous difference at the implementation stage because when things do go wrong, we will be ready for it. An easy way to 'test' our ideas is to imagine that we are physically walking through the new process already in operation. In this manner we can picture all the possible mishaps which might happen with our new design.

The team might show quite a lot of annoyance at the idea of shooting its brand new creation full of holes—but it is essential to the success of the operation. We tackle this part on the second day, when everybody has had a chance to sleep on the new process and can see it with a fresh mind. Several issues will simply 'spring to mind'. Others will need a bit more thought.

TEST AND CHECK, CHECK AND TEST

Flag with a red post-it all the places where our new process is likely to fall down. Be realistic. It is often difficult to question what we have just designed, but in this case it is worth it. If we don't think of it first it will probably happen, and then we will be in *real* trouble.

The aim of the exercise is to be able to implement the new process and get it right *from the moment it starts.* This may sound like wishful thinking but it has been practised spectacularly in several instances, such as the start-up of Tokyo's Disneyworld!

Practical Tip: to kick off the session, start by asking the team to flag the 'technically risky' parts of the new process, steps where we are not totally confident in the robustness of our operations. These areas are usually easy to spot and to remedy.

BARRIERS TO IMPLEMENTATION

Once we have spotted the 'technically risky' areas in the process, we need to think broader and consider the organisational barriers to implementation. These various barriers can be flagged on the board with blue post-its. Most of these barriers will have to do with 'human' factors. Some of these barriers may be politically sensitive, but they are none the less interesting to address so that at the very least everyone can expect a reaction from some quarter or other. Although the softer issues of organisations are seldom expressed explicitly, staff are very aware of them—if not consciously. Most people will have an instant feel for 'what can be done' and what can not. They will also be faced with the structural implications concerning how they will prioritise time and resources. Therefore, many difficult decisions will be accepted as logical on the face of it but are likely to create intense psychological pressure on individuals as they go about implementing the redesign.

Each person will be confronted by a set of limiting factors that are an expression of the structure of the organisation. These factors are usually of a very practical nature—and at the same time hard to express. The main difficulty we have encountered in redesign projects is a situation where we ask someone to either take time off his or her regular job to perform another role or to modify their behaviour. Both requests can be accepted by the person as perfectly logical and legitimate since they are issued by their manager. Yet, they can also appear impossible. The feeling is that they are already over-worked—so how can they be expected to take on yet another role—

and, that the new behaviour asked of them is not only difficult to acquire, but also probably goes against the accepted way of behaving in their peer group. At that stage, ask that they accept on faith that the new behaviour will enable them to perform better so they will have more time for their new role, from which they will gain increased status that will legitimise the new behaviour, and so forth ... None the less we must accept that these requests will create anxiety because, in a way, they go against the behaviour induced by the structure.

LIMITING FACTORS ARE RELATIVE AND DIFFUSE

The difficulty the team will encounter as it tries to highlight these limiting factors is that they vary according to organisations and individuals. Because they are an expression of the structure, they differ from one organisational role or status to another. People have different objectives, responsibilities and constraints—and therefore their sets of limiting factors will be different, linked to their specific position in the structure.

Furthermore, different personalities will have 'preferred' problems: situations they can tackle better than others. Consequently, two different persons in the same organisational position can be confronted by very different limiting factors. This difficulty is accrued by the fact that we are dealing with *perceived* difficulty. The fact that these limiting factors are not formally addressed in the decision-making process means that the individuals have no way to know whether the difficulty they anticipate is realistic or not. In some cases, managers will tend to *ascribe intentions from their own fears* and increase the perceived difficulty of the situation.

Confronted with one of these limiting factors, we can choose to:

■ Go ahead regardless of our fears.
■ Do nothing and wait to see what happens with the other parts of the process.
■ Substitute this task with something we feel would do just as well and which is easier to achieve.

Combined, these behaviours can inflict a considerable drift on a project, and not be noticeable. Because of their very nature, these behaviours will be diffuse: they will express themselves in different, apparently unrelated issues—and as a result not give a consistent picture of what is happening. Faced with this kind of drift no one can ascertain one cause of drift and fix it.

REACTIONS TO CHANGE ARE OFTEN UNEXPECTED

A diplomat once confided that his job was about expecting the worst. Through many years of doing just that, he learnt that the worst never comes as fast as you expect it, it's never as bad as you expect it and it's never in the form that you expect it. Whatever anticipation of reaction managers have, the chances are they will be surprised, because, as we have seen, we are dealing with anticipation.

People tend to expect the reaction they fear most rather than what is most likely to happen. For instance, in managing a redesign project a project manager lived with the fear that people would point-blank refuse to do their part of the work because it conflicted with their own functional priorities. As it turned out, they never did, and the job got done. However, he was having a different problem throughout the period. The overall manager of the department would call the project manager in regularly to tell him to be 'more careful' and to make 'less waves' and so forth. As a change agent, he dismissed such comments as part of the job, until they became rather strong and personal—to the point that he almost stopped everything altogether several times, not knowing what was causing such uproar because the people around him maintained they were quite happy with how the project was developing.

It was only after the project was (successfully) completed that it was possible to understand what had been happening. There was no real problem within the project team itself but the managers of each of the persons involved resented the fact that the cross-functional project was taking precedence over some of their functional priorities. Although the project manager had the authority to run this project, which was considered to have overall importance, several functional managers complained to his manager about their lack of resources, work not getting done, his 'negative influence' on their staff, etc. The manager responsible for the project would then come to him about vague—but strong—complaints that he could not relate to the work itself. Whereas the project manager expected resistance from the work itself, nothing happened. The reaction came from a different angle—and almost stopped him from finishing the project.

We can identify several symptoms of the same kind: things don't get done because there is other pressing work to do (this can also be true); top management withdraws support at the critical moment because they get too much flak from their peers; there is a constant modification of the plan to accommodate 'constraints'; or the project grinds to a halt because one part of it simply doesn't get done. These reactions can stop the project in its tracks because they are hard to link to the project itself—they are seen as external events—and often hard to ignore.

POLISH THE REDESIGN

Taking this information into account, how can we polish our design to deal with the weaker areas? Is there someone else we should speak to? This is where the team must be encouraged to be *creative*. Solutions to problems can be as obvious as giving someone a quick call to warn him or her of a change to come, or as complex as a jazzy new program. The only constraint required from solutions to potential problems is that they must be practical. We don't want to solve one aspect of implementation, simply to create more heartache elsewhere.

DESIGN AN ACTION PLAN

How can we create the *conditions* that will ensure right-first-time implementation? By responding to the numerous barriers to implementation, we can build a robust action plan. Our objective is to identify all the possible actions we could take to resolve a situation. The question we are trying to answer is the following:

> What are the possible actions we can take to create favourable circumstances for this outcome to happen?

The phrasing may sound a bit elaborate, but is key. We want to do more than just 'implement', we want to create the right circumstances so that our new process will be welcomed by the rest of the organisation—not sabotaged. This involves thinking of all the people-issues that might be disregarded in the light of more technical matters. Some of these people-issues, such as warning customers of a change, can be really simple, and yet they are terribly important.

Step 1: Warm up with a team talk exercise. Choose the phrasing of the question addressed.

Step 2: The facilitator writes the 'question' in the top left-hand corner of the board and checks that all the team members agree with the phrasing.

Step 3: Each participant writes his or her answers to the question on cards or post-it notes.

Step 4: The participants place their cards or post-its on the left-hand side of the board.

Step 5: The facilitator takes each individual post-it, places it in the middle of the board and repeats the question. He or she checks that everyone in the group understands what the author of the post-it meant. There is no discussion about agreeing or disagreeing with the content, just a simple check of understanding.

If the group doesn't understand, the facilitator asks the author to re-write the card or post-it, and tries again.

This step can appear heavy-going, but it is absolutely necessary for the effectiveness of the next steps. Each idea must have been considered by the group, and the meaning must have been made clear.

Step 6: Once all the notes have been checked, the whole group comes to the board and regroups the notes according to what seems the most 'intuitive' grouping. Participants can move notes around freely, regardless of where other people have put them before. Each group must include no more than eight notes.

Some notes won't fit in any groups. These outliers can be left on their own as a special case. They should not be 'force integrated' just for the sake of tidiness.

Step 7: The participants give titles to each group, and write this title on a different colour card or post-it. They then gather all the notes of one group under its title, and start forming new groups.

Step 8: At this stage, the groups are unravelled again to appear as a tree:

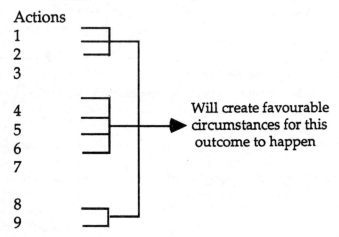

Actions

1
2
3

4
5
6
7

8
9

Will create favourable circumstances for this outcome to happen

Step 9: Each action is ranked in terms of (1) effectiveness or impact, and (2) feasibility. Symbols are used to rank them from Low to High.

Step 10: The most effective and most feasible actions are then chosen and detailed into a 'What Who How When Why Where and at What Cost' Plan, and allocated to team members as 'To Do' actions.

PROGRESS MEETING

In practice what happens is that the relevant actions are allocated around the team. Each person takes responsibility for a set of actions by picking up the post-its from the board and placing them in front of him or her. If there is any time left, the 'What Who How When Why Where and at What Cost' sheets for each action can be drawn up immediately, if not, people take their post-its and draw the plans afterwards.

It can be very helpful to organise a short progress meeting a few days later. At this meeting we simply go round the table and people present their action sheets. A schedule for the implementation can then be designed and last-minute details ironed out.

STEP 6: IMPLEMENT AND STANDARDISE

───────── ✧ ─────────

Just do it. Unfortunately there is no magical recipe for implementation other than getting down to the work. In most projects I have been involved with, the new designs actually made sense and there was never any real problem at the implementation stage. If it doesn't make sense, however, people are not very likely to get moving. The advantage of the detailed preparation which happens in the two-day redesign seminar is that people are quite satisfied with what they need to do, by when. There is not much latitude for not doing it since it would usually block someone else's efforts. In general, team members are actually quite keen to make their design happen and put in the necessary energy to make sure that it does. Problems do appear, but they are mostly expected, and as such, solved with minimal fuss.

DRAW UP AN IMPLEMENTATION BOARD

If the team, or the department manager, has appointed a project manager, he or she can set up an implementation board on the basis of the action plan, to make sure that the redesign keeps on track. As it happens, this is seldom necessary, but can be quite helpful in case of a delay or if some members of the team get bogged down. The board—to be prominently displayed—can look like this:

ACTION	OWNER	BY WHEN	CHECK-UP	COM-MENTS
A brief description of the action	Who is supposed to make it happen	Deadline	An appointment to check how things are going before the deadline	Comments
Action 1	Sylvia	15/6/95	5/6/95	
Action 2	Peter	16/6/95	4/6/95	

KEEP A LOG

It is also good practice to keep a log book of the implementation. This will help to keep it on track, but is also a very useful source for further analysis. In particular, specific solutions will be recorded that can be applied to other similar problems. Furthermore, this log book will give a record of why such and such policies were put in place, which can help to reduce the lead-time by 50 per cent when we come back to the same process. The log book should show:

■ The original process flow-chart.
■ The redesigned process flow-chart.
■ The action board.
■ Comments from customers and colleagues after implementation.

QUALITY IS IN THE STANDARD

From a customer's point of view, being able to count on what the team will deliver is the first step of quality. Unreliability, even if it sometimes delivers outstanding work, creates an uncertainty that is difficult to handle for most customers. The first necessary step to improve our service is to narrow down the dispersion of our output: to get as close as possible to a standard.

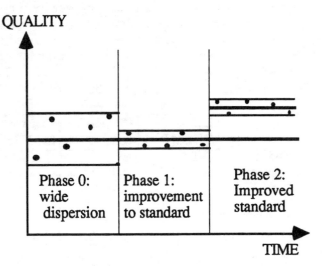

After the redesigned process has been put in place, a persistent effort must be maintained to make sure that the new process produces standardised results. If it works one time but not the other, the Walk-through/Talk-through and action plan sessions need to be run again, till the process is brought under control.

DEVELOP BEST PRACTICE CHECKLISTS

Once we are satisfied that the process is under control, we want to draw up best practice checklists (BPC) for each step. This is a friendly name for an operating procedure. The idea is that to maintain the process at its current standard and not let it slip, we want to set it in the form of a series of procedures for each step. These procedures—in practice, checklists—become the organisational know-how on how to produce this particular output.

To create a BPC book for the process, we return to the process map. Under each step, we detail each operation in terms of physical movements.

Step 1

Break down each step into detailed instructions. Create diagrams for difficult tasks. Provide examples.

Step 2

Write the *main steps* by identifying the main action. Not all the steps are critical or need to be detailed; it is only important to focus on the main steps.

Step 3

Write the key checkpoints by identifying the key specifications. How do I know I'm doing the right thing?

Step 4

Summarise steps 2 and 3 in a checklist by:

- Trying the instructions.
- Arguing it out.
- Agreeing on the instructions.

CUSTOMER CARE

Customer care is about more than providing an adequate service 'because they haven't got anywhere else to go to'. Fundamentally, we need to find out how we can reasonably satisfy more of the customer's needs. To quote Will Rogers: 'Even if you are on the right track, you'll get run over if you just sit there'. Like it or not, we need to keep moving ahead. To get on the right track we need to define key items of customer satisfaction. We can define these items from the information gathered in the Customer's Requirements table. These key customer needs can then be represented as a 'tree':

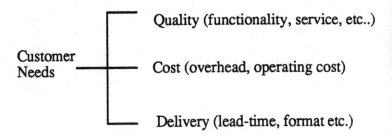

Customer Needs
- Quality (functionality, service, etc..)
- Cost (overhead, operating cost)
- Delivery (lead-time, format etc.)

ADDRESS CUSTOMERS' NEEDS

There are a variety of ways in which we can deal with customers' needs. The following matrix can help us to plan the way ahead:

APPROACHES TO ADDRESS THE CUSTOMERS' NEEDS

		Upgrade Skills (i.e. follow BPCs)	Problem Solving (i.e. make suggestions)	Leadership (i.e. Provide Recognition)	Management Systems (i.e. Set goals, follow through plans
CUSTOMER NEEDS	Quality				
	Cost				
	Delivery				
	Safety				
	Morale				

PREPARE THE NEXT REDESIGN EFFORT

Thinking about customer care and needs is a way to prepare the next step in our process improvement approach. Once our process is nicely controlled, we must consider running a second redesign workshop to reduce the lead-time a further 50 per cent, and so on, until the process can really happen all in one go, without interfering with other tasks. One can wonder why this deeper thought about customer care hasn't happened earlier. The truth is that any detailed thinking about customer needs, which happens before the process has been tackled seriously, creates castles in the sky because none of the team members has yet developed a truly detailed and operational understanding of the process. In the first redesign effort, customer requirements were implicit in our choices and trade-offs during the redesign. After having done it once, we can be more structured in our thinking about customer care, allowing us to be more rigorous in our *next* redesign effort.

THE 'CUSTOMERS' NEEDS' TRAP

I want to be very clear on one point: all our efforts have only one ultimate objective: better customer service. The problem is that if you kick off any meeting with the question 'what does the customer really want from us?', you might as well go home for the evening. Every time I've seen this happen, a strenuous discussion arises about what the customer might or might not want—all these wishes being both contradictory and extreme. As we noted before, the 'client' is usually made up of several different customers who will want different things. Very often the client firm or department is itself unclear about its own needs and priorities. In this situation we can end up talking for hours without ever doing anything.

The way out of this dilemma is to be pragmatic. Assume for a start that the client wants more of the same but better, and work from there. Better usually means:

- More reliable.
- Cheaper.
- Faster.
- More personalised.

The specifics of how much cheaper is cheaper, or what kind of personalisation is essential and what is 'nice to have', cannot be determined at the outset. We must start our redesign work from simple assumptions of what the customer wants, and then, as we make our choices, check with their priorities. As a rule, if we do something they really don't like they'll tell us. The trick is to ask them first. 'How would you feel if we did less of A and more of B?' The answer will be Yes, No or Indifferent, which is usually enough to tell us whether to proceed in that direction or not. As you redesign your process for the second or third time, the customer will be far more aware of what you are doing and involved in the exercise. They'll tell you what they want.

CASE STUDY: PUMPCO

This short case study will describe the process redesign approach in situation. The process I will present is typical of a 'first try choice'. It is important, it creates constant hassle and yet it is not critical to the business. As such, it made a perfect learning experience for the company, which has tackled more critical processes since.

Pumpco is an industrial pump manufacturer. They build about 100 pumps a day and service a variety of industrial clients. Their main problem was answering customer modification requests (CMR). Although not essential, this process was a constant sore point in commercial relationships with customers. In 1993, the company's design department received 950 customer modification requests. It managed to process 259 of these demands. There was an ongoing debate between the design manager who considered that the company accepted far too many modification requests from customers, and the sales manager who argued that the modification process simply took too long. In the end, the managing director decided to focus a redesign effort on the modification's processing time. Since the mid-1980s, a 'Project Management' structure had been created to co-ordinate all work between designers, engineers and production. This structure used a computer project management software package to keep track of progress. Project management's role was mainly administrative.

The team was formed in late November, and was expected to have a new process in place for the New Year. Some members of the team were familiar with business re-engineering concepts, others had received problem-solving training. The team decided to do the walk-through as a group: as several members of the team were actually part of the process, they took one modification request and showed the others what work was actually needed at each stage. The overall estimation of the current lead-time was 120 working days per modification.

The team then went through the two-day workshop and drew up the following process.

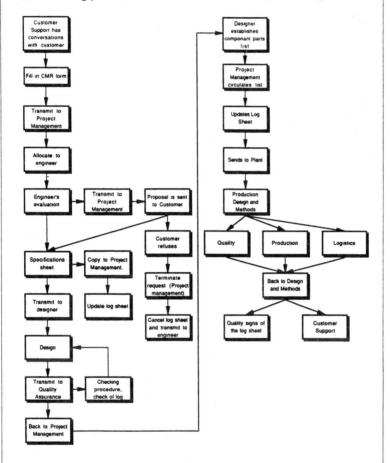

This was estimated to give the following order of time:

	Value-Added time	Real Time
Conversations	1	1
Project management	1	1
Engineer	3	15

Programme manager	5	37
Designer	10	32
Quality	10	35
Project management	1	1
Designer	1	4
Project management	2	7
Manufacturing plant	5	10
Total	39	143

In the redesign phase, the team decided to:

1. Create a fast track for simple modifications.
2. Suppress unnecessary steps.
3. Parallel process the information flows.

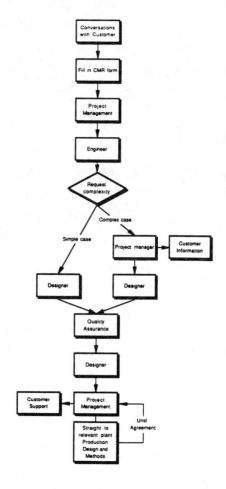

The implementation turned out to be rather easy, and the results were spectacular. In February 1994, it appeared that the modifications were processed in a week for the simple problems, and, at the utmost, five weeks for the complex ones. The number of modifications accepted was also soon brought down because the engineers derived a better understanding from their redesign work of what kind of modification would take how long—rather than focusing on the most 'challenging' ones as they used to. All in all, the company managed to process most of its backlog through 1994 and started 1995 with a clean slate.

9

PROCESS IMPROVEMENT PLAN

What next? If we have satisfactorily redesigned our first process, where do we go from here? Most of the time, the first redesign experiment is conducted on a process which addresses a problem but is not critical to the business. In this way, we can solve a real problem without taking much of a risk. Yet, how do we apply the learning achieved from this first experience? Process redesign actually gives us a formidable tool to progressively 'tighten up' our entire operation. If the first exercise is reactive—we solve a problem—once the tool is in hand we can start using it pro-actively. In essence, process redesign is a technique we can apply to entire business areas to progressively bring them 'under control'.

Control is not to be taken in the traditional sense of 'control and command' but that of statistical control. The redesign exercise leads to standardisation of our activity, and in doing so we acquire a precise understanding of the cause and effect relationships at work on the process. From then on we can really act, not just react, through modifying these relationships. Such action guarantees that the process won't 'slip back' into dysfunction after the original improvement. As we are able to keep this constant pressure, we take the first step of the on-going continuous improvement journey.

START CLOSE TO THE CUSTOMER

Which process shall we focus on to start progressively redesigning our entire operation? The obvious starting point will be the processes closest to the customer. By redesigning those processes first we can:

- Leverage direct value for the customer.
- Integrate more fully the customer's point of view.

To understand which processes are 'close to the customer' we must consider the entire value chain of the industry. What is the next step in transforming our output into customer value? The processes we need to focus on are those of producing and delivering which directly impact upon the customer's own workflows.

IT'S A 'PULL' SYSTEM: MOVE UPSTREAM

From then on the idea is to establish a 'pull' system. As we redesign and improve the processes closest to the customer, we usually put strain on the next tier processes. In practice, it means that if our end-point process is more streamlined, has less variability and moves faster, the bottleneck will be pushed back one rung of the ladder. Variability coming from upstream will now be an issue, as will be delays and confusion. This movement upstream might create a bit of a panic because many departments which have never been in direct contact with the customer and whose operations have never been seriously questioned will suddenly come under great pressure—from their own internal customers.

Interestingly enough, this is a problem that the two industrial giants of this century had to face, and solved in very different ways. At the root of Henry Ford's success with low cost production was standardised work. He benefited from technological advances both in machine tools and materials which enabled him to use standard parts. Before the first conveyor was even dreamed up, Ford and his team had hit upon the idea of using the same gauge to produce standard parts. This eliminated their greatest bottleneck: the fitting work of one non-standard part to another, which had to be performed by specialised craftsmen at each assembly stage. As the operation grew and Ford started outsourcing, he was soon confronted by the impossibility of finding suppliers who could provide the same degree of standardisation. Characteristically, Ford then started integrating all supplier operations and imposing his production system so that their output could be used by his assembly operation—in the process creating the monstrous Rouge complex.

When Taichi Ohno started to develop lean production at Toyota, the firm soon hit a similar problem. Its own very tight Just-in-Time, zero defects system could only operate as long as the supplier could provide timely quality parts. Toyota solved its problem in a very different way, by sending its own engineers to train their suppliers in using the Toyota Production System. Toyota benefited because it got the parts it needed when it needed them and the supplier benefited because it gained the considerable competitive advantage of operating the Toyota System. The symbiosis reinforced itself as ex-Toyota people would often find work with their first-tier suppliers. In turn, the suppliers started training their own suppliers until the entire industry chain shaped up to Toyota's exacting standards.

HALVE THE LEAD-TIME, AGAIN AND AGAIN

Each redesigned process should show an improvement of 50 per cent lead-time at the very least. Yet, in order for this step-change to be maintained it must be understood that this 50 per cent gain is only the first step. After about 6 to 12 months, once the process has been standardised, a second redesign workshop needs to be run to reduce the lead-time by another 50 per cent. This may seem just as incredible as the first time but it is just as feasible. The same principles apply, time and time again. There is always a way to make operations simpler!

Continuous improvement guru Ishikawa was recently visiting a Japanese automotive plant in the UK. Long gone was the time when tool changes were brought down from six hours to two; then from two hours to half an hour; then from half an hour to ten minutes; and finally from ten minutes to the one minute it takes the operator simply to shift a turntable around and place the other tool. The plant's engineers were very nervous because, as they explained to the master, they couldn't find any further improvement to make to their operation. He maintained many things could still be improved. Finally, he had his improvement team sit in front of a machine whilst it was operating. The brief was simple. Sit there in silence, with no pen and paper, watching the machine operate until someone comes up with an improvement. The team watched the machine for two hours before it dawned on them that there were further improvements to make. This realisation led them to change, once more, much of their thinking about production processes and make some further radical changes to the plant.

Once you get a good idea of the sequence of dependent processes, you can establish a redesign timetable to plan the redesign of your operation:

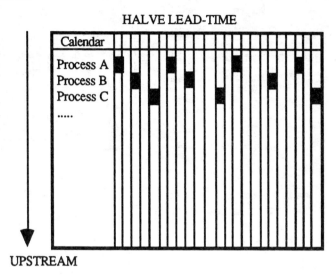

SIMPLIFY, SIMPLIFY, SIMPLIFY

The fundamental rule we follow in process redesign is that of simplification. Operations must be simplified, not on paper, but for the people who actually do the job. Anything that makes their work easier is good for the process. In fact, the more we simplify each individual step in the process, the more we gain in flexibility. At the end of the day, we want to be in the position of using ten people to do one task each if the demand is high or one person performing one task if the demand is low.

Suppose your customer demand is five per day, and that you have four steps in your process with one person per step. Each person does five per day, which altogether produces five items per day.

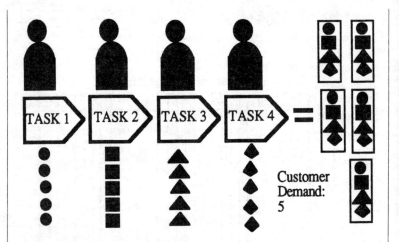

However, if demand falls to one per day, you still need to perform the four steps of the process for a finished output. Ideally you want to be in a position where one person can do each of the fours steps in turn to deliver the demand:

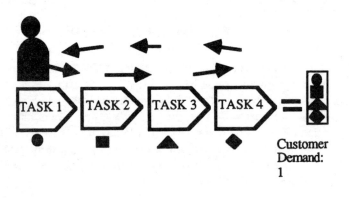

In order to achieve this goal, each step must be so simple that it can be performed by the same person. What is more, the process *itself* must be simple enough to be followed by the same person. Although this aim might seem totally unrealistic at the moment, it is at the heart of the 'flexible enterprise' dream. Flexibility in general can only be achieved through flexibility at the task level.

KEEP AN EYE OUT FOR CUT CORNERS

In redesign work the old notion of 'value for money' keeps reappearing when least expected. If people find a 'clever' solution which will enable them to kill two birds with one stone, they will probably implement it—and be thoroughly pleased with themselves. The organisation will probably even reward them for it. However, watch out. Many such solutions in fact create further process entanglements, which can become extremely difficult to resolve later.

Keep processes independent

A typical cut-corner is to push back two flows into the same process. In effect, this re-creates dependence. Once dependence is re-established, we run into the usual fragmentation and queuing problems. Yet, in most situations, the flexibility needed for actually responding to demand is not there. The temptation is then to send another job through a process when the process has a lower workload. This convenient short-term solution soon turns sour as the original work picks up. What happens is that people tend to discount variability. Workloads are not constant but vary around an average.

For instance, suppose that we have the previous process working at full capacity for a while:

	TASK 1	TASK 2	TASK 3	TASK 4	Demand
Items	5	5	5	5	5

If demand drops, we then get the following situation:

	TASK 1	TASK 2	TASK 3	TASK 4	Demand
Items	3	3	3	3	3
Capacity	2	2	2	2	0

This free time could then be used to run a second workflow through the same process:

Flow A	TASK 1	TASK 2	TASK 3	TASK 4	Demand
Items	3	3	3	3	3

Flow B	TASK 1*	TASK 2*	TASK 3*	TASK 4*	Demand
Items	2	2	2	2	2

Such a system could well work if each workflow was in control, but with normal variability we can expect demand for both flows A and B to vary. Demand for A could be 3, back to 5 or down to 1. There is no reason to expect demand for B to remain stable at 2. It could easily move to 1, or 3. Supposing that at some point both variabilities move up at the same time, demand for A is back to 5, and demand for B is up to 4.

Flow A	TASK 1	TASK 2	TASK 3	TASK 4	Demand
Items	5	5	5	5	5
Flow B	TASK 1*	TASK 2*	TASK 3*	TASK 4*	Demand
Items	4	4	4	4	4
TOTAL	9	9	9	9	9

Some hard choices will have to be made. What happens then is that each person will try to juggle around with their schedule so that it 'sort of works'. The idea is to do a bit of A now, and then some of B, and so forth. As we do this, the entire process suddenly loses considerable effectiveness. The time spent at each task session can easily double simply from the interruption of one type of work to the next, and the overall backlog will increase immediately without any apparent solution to the process. The lesson is to *keep processes independent*.

Each process should happen in one go

In many cases, particularly with administrative work, there is no way to dedicate a team to one particular operation. Several workflows have to go through the same physical process. In this case, we will try to segregate the work flows so that they happen in sequence, not intermingled with each other. In doing so we gain considerable efficiency by re-establishing a natural order of work.

People are often accused of procrastinating. Procrastination happens because it is difficult to move from one task to another. You have to find it, get into it and so forth. So, at each change of type of work we are quite likely to procrastinate. There is nothing wrong with that. Usually it annoys us more than anyone else because it means longer hours before going home. To avoid these 'procrastination traps' the best thing is to try to change the type of work infrequently. This way, one will want to run different workflows in succession, rather than doing a bit of one, then a bit of another, and so forth.

It's OK to have a bit of over-capacity

Don't worry too much about having a bit of spare capacity—especially with equipment. If demand on a process falls, the utilisation time of its equipment falls with it, but don't try to optimise it again by 'giving it more things to do'. You might optimise locally, but it is quite clear that this won't help get more products out of your gates and to the client. At best you'll create some stock somewhere, and at worst you could slow down all operations by creating a bottleneck somewhere else in the system at a critical point.

DON'T CREATE PROCESS TEAMS—THE TEAMS ARE *AD HOC*

A common temptation when doing regular process redesign work is to create a permanent redesign team whose function will be to 'go around and redesign processes'. This temptation must be resisted at all costs for a variety or reasons:

- First, by creating a permanent team, you also will have to deal with all the classical issues of team performance that you can easily avoid with *ad hoc* teams put together for a brief period of time on a very specific task, ie a redesign.
- You will also create a specialised body who will increasingly feel that it knows better than the people actually doing the job, and be more reluctant to invite them to sessions. In those sessions the operational people will be faced with a coherent team, with its own habits and, to a certain degree, its own culture, and might be reluctant to co-operate. It is far more effective to pull operational people out of their jobs for the time it takes to do one specific restructuring. It also gives the team an incentive to get on with it because work will be piling up on their desks.
- Finally, such a team would become institutionalised, and what started off as a project team might well end up a permanent process analysis group. There is always only one short step from being part of the solution to being part of the problem.

TRAIN PROCESS REDESIGN COACHES

You might, however, want to train a few specialised redesign 'coaches', who could take charge of the redesign exercises. These few people (no more than one per plant or department) could:

■ Act as facilitators in the redesign exercises.
■ Baby-sit the team throughout implementation.
■ Become process experts.

There is, of course, always more to understanding redesign, and it is a lot to ask of someone who already has a line job to do. Being a Process Coach for a year is a perfect job for a young manager waiting to be promoted to broader responsibilities. By taking him or her out of the line role for a year, they will gain much experience in how things actually work in diverse areas of the business as well as a strong sense of the effects of policies on workflows, which would hold them in good stead for future management roles.

KILL-DATE FOR PROCESSES

As part of the restructuring effort we want to keep processes progressing on an operational level. Many management thinkers blame all the ills of organisations on old, unchallenged assumptions about 'the way we do things'. To avoid this, it can be very stimulating to set a kill-date to any process you have. At that date (about two to five years) this process will simply be terminated, and we then need to find something radically different to replace it—if the job still needs doing. This discipline can be a driving force for organisational progress. It provides a simple way to institutionalise change as a 'normal' part of running the business. We understand it, we master it.

The software design department of a large software house gave a further twist to this idea by developing competing processes when the kill-date would approach. A second team would be working on the same process and its mission was to come up with a radically innovative process at the same place. Such an attitude keeps the strong 'pioneering' spirit of the company alive, as well as producing quite stunning and innovative results.

LOOK OUT FOR OLD PROCESSES TO ERADICATE

Organisations are literally created by an accumulation of processes over time. First we do this, then that, and so on. Each of these 'processes' is represented by a 'rule', 'policy' or simply the injunction 'we've always done it this way'. Our working environment is cluttered with tasks which were inscribed into the system simply because they were 'a good idea at the time'. Many of these things don't make sense anymore, but we are still loath to do away with them. Be ruthless: get rid of any repetitive task which doesn't seem to make sense!

Practical Tip: get rid of all procedures which are humiliating for staff or customers!

In a similar manner, look out for processes which are humiliating for staff or customers. The notions of what is OK and what is not change with time, and such things as reserved parking spaces, uniformed attendants during business lunches, and many other privileges are increasingly out of place in a modern environment. The main issue is that many of these policies are humiliating to staff—which is bad for morale—or to customers—which is bad for sales. For instance, many complaints procedures are an excruciating process from the customer's point of view. A disappointed customer who could let off steam through an easy complaint procedure might come back. One who couldn't even have his or her say won't. Such humiliating procedures are still occurring in our processes and are often ignored! Look out for them and get rid of them immediately.

During a redesign workshop in a French hospital, nurses started wondering why they had to distribute thermometers to all patients at precisely 6a.m. every morning. This was a particularly unwelcome procedure since it involved waking up people who, by and large, would have been far better off asleep. It turned out that no-one knew why thermometer distribution had to happen at this hour since the results were only gathered at least two hours later! The only reason which came to mind was: 'We've always done it like this.'

RESTRUCTURE AS YOU GO

What about all this restructuring we hear so much about in business process re-engineering? As I mentioned earlier, there are great dangers to restructuring up front, without working first at task level. As you redesign various processes, however, many organisational aberrations will come to light. Restructuring happens as we go. On a sensible operational basis we can change the shape of the organisation without simply moving boxes around, or changing the names in the boxes.

When restructuring, remember career paths. The greatest danger to a new structure is to be shunned by promising people because they see it as a dead end. On the contrary, the best thing to happen is for that structure to be seen as a stepping stone for better and bigger things. When restructuring, always keep an eye out for the potential implications of the change on standard career paths. This could have a very strong impact on the success of your structure in the years to come.

BUILD A CROSS-FUNCTIONAL ORGANISATION

The ultimate goal is to rebuild the organisation entirely according to process principles. This, of course, is what the big consultancies argue can be done through full-scale re-engineering efforts—yet, think of the pain! By taking our time, we can change the organisation without trauma. We can also deal with the main practical problems which crop up. What should the new organisation look like? The best model we find at the moment is that of the cross-functional organisation. Cross-functional management (CFM) has been defined as 'a management process designed to encourage and support interdepartmental communication and co-operation throughout the company'.[10] The purpose is to attain such company-wide targets as quality, cost, and delivery of products and services by optimising the sharing of work.

In all likelihood, CFM began at Toyota in the late 1950s and early 1960s. Toyota's senior management felt the need to compete on a different basis: they would endeavour to use management effectiveness (people) as a tool for strategic advantage rather than capital intense investments (equipment). A breakthrough in the approach was the development of a new category of company-wide functions, managed by senior line-managers—in addition to their functional responsibilities—to build a company-wide knowledge team in key areas. Over the years this system was refined within the Toyota group and has been widely applied in Japan. CFM has begun to be implemented in the US, for example at Cummins Engine, Ford, Kodak and Hewlett-Packard.

Unfortunately, there is no easy way to construct a CFM system. As we pointed out earlier, people need a functional 'home' to further their own careers, and 'process management' is simply too general. Furthermore, in organising around processes, we run the risk of recreating the traditional 'matrix structure' and finding everybody at each other's throat within one month of the announcement of the new structure.

A large US-based company went through a full-scale re-engineering effort to become more customer focused. As a result of the re-organisation, 'cross-functional' roles were created. These jobs were set in place to improve co-operation in a traditional and political structure. However, after a few months, it turned out that internal political wars waged stronger than ever. Upon analysis, it was shown that the organisation had fallen into one of the classic pitfalls of matrix structures: the cross-functional managers had large financial resources (budgets) but few human resources (people). Conversely, the line managers had plenty of staff, but no money—since the budgets had been diverted towards cross-functional roles. As a result, getting things done depended on a continual play of fragile alliances.

How can we build a true cross-functional organisation? Each company must find its own careful compromise. However, there are certain principles which can be helpful to guide restructuring *as we go*.

Organise around processes, not tasks

From a pragmatic point of view, it is obvious that we want to organise work around processes, rather than individual tasks. However, functions and specialisation are bound to be organised around tasks, rather than processes. At this stage, it is important to separate *management* from *operational supervision*. Management is a generalist problem, it only concerns the senior levels of the organisation. Operational supervision is about supervising the people actually doing the work—which can remain function based. Management takes decisions, supervisors implement them. If we make this distinction, we can keep a traditional functional organisation up to supervisory level, and then switch to a process-based organisation at managerial level.

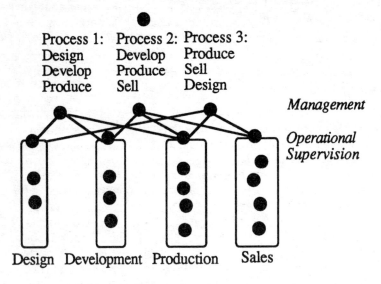

Process 1:
Design
Develop
Produce

Process 2:
Develop
Produce
Sell

Process 3:
Produce
Sell
Design

Management

Operational Supervision

Design Development Production Sales

Such a structure puts the operational supervisor under pressure, since he or she will have to deal with several 'bosses'. However, being responsible for processes as opposed to functions, the managers will also be under pressure to co-operate in the demands they make of the supervisors, and present unified requests.

In order to jump the gap between supervision and management, a supervisor would need experience in several functional jobs, so as to understand enough of the specifics to be able to see the 'big picture' at process level. Careers happen functionally at first, then cross-functionally. Since we are dealing with a limited number of people at the cross-functional level, career development issues are far less important.

Flatten the hierarchy

The fastest growing thing in any organisation always seems to be its hierarchy. There are always more managers than people to manage, and endless games about how to move these managers around the structure so that the imbalance won't show too much. Intuitively, having more chiefs than indians doesn't make much sense. Interestingly enough, this is a fairly recent problem. Many pre-World War II organisations employed thousands of people with as few as five hierarchical levels. Old-timers describe sites such as those of the Great Western Railway with hundreds of people reporting directly to one person. Endless numbers of 'managers' started appearing as people took the concept of *span-of-control* seriously.

In the 1960s, a rumour spread through the business world which argued that to manage effectively, a manager could only deal with six to nine subordinates at a time. This remarkable piece of knowledge blatantly flies in the face of humanity's greatest organised achievements, from the pyramids to the railway networks. However, it makes some kind of sense, particularly when one is not too good at managing: six to nine people is about as many as we can handle *easily*. In the first chapter, we compared the structure of an American plant and a Japanese plant. The American plant boasted 135 support staff for 107 direct staff. The Japanese plant had only seven support staff to show for 50 direct staff—guess who is actually more effective at managing? Yet, it is hardly surprising. Suppose you have 100 workers and want to create a management structure with a six-to-one span of control. You will need about 17 supervisors for 100 workers. The 17 supervisors will need 3 managers to supervise them. Three managers who will need a production director to supervise them in turn. All in all, you need 21 people to manage 100—about 20 per cent—without even counting all the 'support' these managers will need (at least a secretary per manager) and so forth. Why not have one person supervise the one hundred? Impossible! No—it used to be done all the time. Each team can easily have a team leader who does not have supervisory status, and still works on the output. The teams, let us say 10 teams of 10 people, can easily be managed by one person—as opposed to 20.

> **Practical Tip: Ignore the six-to-nine required span of control. Organise your hierarchy according to the level of work and responsibility, not number of people.**

Psychologist Eliott Jaques argues that there is a psychological measure to 'real' hierarchical authority. According to his research, people will only accept the authority of someone whose tasks are considerably longer than theirs. He argues that the only reliable measure of the 'level of work' of a role is its 'time-span':[b1]

> Any task has both a what to be accomplished (the output, goal, objective) and a by-when. The what is the particular output which is to be achieved. The by-when is the longest maximum-target-completion-time set by the manager for that particular output.

> The longest of the maximum-target-completion-times of tasks in the role give a direct measure of the level of work of the role. I call this measure the Time-Span of Discretion of the role (time-span). The time-span is an objective fact, since it is derived from an objectively stated decision of a manager. The longer the time-span, the higher the level of work. Any two roles with the same time-span regardless of occupation have the same level of work.

According to this time-span measure, one can define objective levels of authority—regardless of occupation. Jaques proposes that people consider their 'real' manager to be at least one time-span category removed from their own:

- Everyone in a role below 3-months time-span feels the occupant of the first role above 3-months time-span to be the real manager. This is the step from worker to supervisor.
- Between 3-months and 1-year time-span the occupant of the first role above the 1-year time-span is felt to be the real manager. At this level we find first-line managers.
- Between 1-year and 2-year time-span the occupant of the first role above the 2-year time-span is felt to be the real manager. Here we step from first-line to unit managers. Up to 2-year time-span, we are in the operations domain.
- Between 2-year and 5-year time-span the occupant of the first role above the 5-year time-span is felt to be the real manager. At this level, we find General Managers. We have shifted from operations to generalist management.

■ Between 5-year and 10-year time-span the occupant of the first role above the 10-year time-span is felt to be the real manager. From 5 to 10 years time-span, we find Business Unit Presidents. Over 10 years is purely strategic, and the role is one of corporate CEO.

This time-span ladder has the advantage of not referring to span-of-control. A first-line manager can supervise many roles below the 3-months time-span. In building organisations, we have to be careful not to place arbitrary levels which do not fall within the time-span categories. They will not be psychologically relevant to the people within the hierarchy, and will bring their load of confusion and overhead.

Keep a team focus

The key to flatter hierarchies is definitely a better use of *teams*. Well organised teams don't need as much management as a collection of individuals—they can manage themselves. It is therefore advisable to use teams, rather than individuals, as organisational building blocks. The teams you want to create come in two categories:

■ *Permanent work teams*: these teams are mostly functional. They create an organisation for groups of staff working on one part of the process. These teams can be organised around a team-leader who is part of the workflow, with additional responsibilities. They are further structured by clear objectives and regular co-ordination meetings.

■ Ad hoc *cross-functional teams*: at a more managerial level, these teams are not permanent. They are formed on an *ad hoc* basis to deal with specific situations which come up in the course of business. They work as 'task forces' and attach themselves to specific problems or opportunities. They are not permanent because we don't want to create yet one more level of bureaucracy—but they can still have a long-term existence if their purpose warrants it.

In order to make the teams *work*, remember to:

■ Give clear team objectives. These objectives need to be specific and quantified (eg, two reports per month, zero customer complaints per week, etc)

- Reward team performance, not just individual performance. Rewards can be both financial (bonus) or psychological (praise). Don't point towards individuals for praise or blame but rather to the entire team.
- Develop multiple competencies. They should be the norm, not the exception. This often relies on deliberate training and information exchange.

More supplier–customer contact

When all is said and done, we still don't talk enough to our customers. We haven't got the time, the access, or even the desire to do so. Yet the customer is our only source of relevant feedback on how we do our job. Although we are confronted with endless difficulties, such as differentiating our customers within our client base (the purchasing officer is not the one who actually uses our work), the rewards are well worth the effort. From an organisational point of view, the main difficulty is providing staff with the opportunity to talk to the customer. This usually means time away from their desk, travelling expenses and so on. Yet, time away from the desk can still be work! The organisation must make it easy for staff to talk to customers.

Reflecting on his time spent with Seiko instruments, John Rehfeld shares his experience of working with a Japanese company:[12]

> I was amazed at how easily the Japanese would jump on an airplane to visit a customer. I could always get the president of Toshiba America to fly to Texas, even for a one-hour meeting. I do my share of flying too. Recently, I flew from California to Greenville, South Carolina for one two-hour meeting.

> At Seiko Instruments, we have guidelines for how much time we should spend visiting customers, either at their offices or at trade shows, and we tie customer contacts to the management bonus plan, even for top managers. General management should spend 20% of its time with customers, for instance; sales management 40%, operations management 30%, field service management 20%, marketing 25%, and engineering 5%. This is one way to reinforce the idea that customers matter.

Practical Tip: Seiko's guidelines for time spent visiting customers:

General Management	20% of its time
Sales Management	40% of its time
Operations Management	30% of its time
Field Service Management	20% of its time
Marketing	25% of its time
Engineering	5% of its time

While CFM is the exception rather than the rule in Japanese companies, it is practised in firms such as Toyota, Komatsu and Pentel. In each company the implementation is slightly different, but the common theme is that there are cross-functional committees that are supported by staff of functional departments. Cross-functional committees make decisions that are then implemented by the staff of the committee, or make recommendations to senior management or the board. These recommendations are then approved by the board or senior management and implemented by the cross-functional committee staff.

WHAT ABOUT TOP MANAGEMENT'S ROLE?

There is one thing all authors on change management agree upon: the key to organisational change is top management commitment. Unfortunately, management and most particularly 'top management' is seldom committed to change. This invariably explains why so many change programmes flounder or downright disappear. This, of course, is true as far as it goes. No matter how successful, pragmatic or courageous the changes you implement, if top management doesn't back them, sooner or later things will revert to how they were before—if not worse.

This does not mean that one needs top management support to get started. In practice, quite spectacular process improvement can happen locally at one manager's initiative—to the utmost dismay, confusion and guilt of the rest of the management structure. But to get those changes built into the organisation, or implemented more widely, top management participation is essential, up to director level. What can management provide?

Resources

There is no easy way to change an organisation. Sooner or later one needs resources, either in budgets (training, material, etc) or in people. The innovative manager can go a long way in the wheeling-dealing-bullying-scrounging approach of the entrepreneur, but this will only take him or her so far. At some point, when all possible favours have been cashed in, he or she will need managerial approval (we supported her all along) or risk being ostracised.

Method and rigour

Management commitment is not simply about providing resources. Management can also bring a method for change, and make sure it is applied with *rigour*. Once local experiments are fully understood and 'under control' they need to be explained to the rest of the company. This can be 'touch and go'. Top management can help by devising a method for implementation, and then see that it is enforced with rigour. There is nothing more disconcerting than a business where some parts have perfectly understood the move forward, whilst others are still moving backwards. Rigour is necessary to implement the new principles.

> A French car manufacturer's senior production team was trying to understand why it couldn't catch up with its main Japanese competitor. They had understood all the principles of JIT, Kanban, SPC. They knew the methods. But still, they couldn't implement them as well as they wanted. Finally, they came to realise that, for their Japanese competitor, principles such as 'right first time', 'zero stock', 'respect of all employees' were not simply guidelines but actually 'golden rules' which were enforced with a surprising degree of ruthlessness.

Objectives and indicators

One of the ways top management can enforce rigour is by establishing clear indicators for the new processes. These indicators, in turn, become firm objectives for local managers, who will be held accountable. The methods must be freely available (training, consultants, in-house experts) so that local managers can actually work to reach those objectives.

Practical Tip: here are typical indicators in a production system:

- Sales per person.
- Inventory on sales.
- Measures of machine performance (up-time) or for team-work.
- The number of people involved in problem-solving groups.
- The number of suggestions per person.
- The average ability to operate different jobs.

To use a Boston Consulting Group[13] formula, the ultimate aim of re-engineering is to trigger a 'paradigm shift' for management from:

Measure the process, manage the results

to

Manage the process, measure the results

CASE STUDY: THE PRISON SERVICE

On some occasions, senior management *is* the driving force behind the re-engineering effort. In such cases, the project takes the form of 'textbook re-engineering': designing new organisation and structure, downsizing headcount, becoming customer focused, and so forth. Yet, even in these cases, particular care has to be taken to involve task level staff in order to make the new structure 'work'. Here is an example of a fairly 'classical' re-engineering in the public sector.

From February 1993 through to February 1994, top consultant Richard Elsner led the Kinsley Lord consulting team in an assignment which helped the Industries and Farms Division of the Prison Service in the UK to transform its organisation, from a command-and-control functional organisation to that of a service supplier to the operating line, organised around key processes. In a review by Parliament in 1994 of the cost effectiveness of consultancy in the UK public service, this project was singled out for special praise. At the end of the year-long process, the outcome was:

- improvements in service level to line customers;
- substantial gains in efficiency and quality of working life;
- reduction in staff costs of up to 30% (£1 million).

In early 1993, the top team of the Prison Service Industries and Farms Division (PSIF) decided to transform the way their head-quarters division was organised and worked so as to respond to major pressures for change within the Prison Service as a whole. First, the key executive body of the service (the Prison's Board) had decided to make a major shift in the allocation of operational power in the organisation: within two years, account-ability for all essential operating decisions would be devolved from headquarters to the operating units, the prisons. Therefore, the role of headquarters divisions (excepting the policy-making and control functions) would need to be transformed signifi-cantly—from a command-and-control role to a service-providing one, responding effectively to the prisons' needs (their customers). Secondly, a major strand of UK government policy was to make its public service more efficient; in the Prison Ser-vice, all headquarters functions were pressurised to make pow-erful cost reductions (usually no less than 50%), principally by cutting their headcount.

The phase of the change involving intensive reorganisation and downsizing stretched over 12 months, until February 1994, when the switch-over to the new organisation took place. Since that time, the new team-based organisation has continued to improve the quality of services it delivers and the internal pro-cesses employed.

The 12-month programme was divided in two phases: a first phase of organisation definition, and a second of process refine-ment, training and staff selection and counselling. One of the key features of the programme throughout was the high level of PSIF staff consultation and involvement, which grounded the work in reality and ensured that the new organisation and ways of working would be both acceptable and practical. The key focus of the change was a re-engineering of the processes em-ployed to deliver customer satisfaction, and a re-building of the structures of work and organisation to 'house' those processes.

In the first phase, a representative sample of PSIF's customers, including high, medium and low security prisons, and prisons for young offenders and women, were consulted, principally on a qualitative basis. This survey identified their perceptions of the evolving needs for support to enable them to run industrial workshops and agricultural enterprises in their establishments, and their expectations of headquarter's functions such as PSIF.

The core services required were distilled from the survey and the key processes for delivery identified. A rough-cut assessment of efficiency and effectiveness of those processes (when they existed) was conducted using panels of employees and customers. Then a full scale redesign of the architecture of PSIF was undertaken, starting from the core processes and aligning them to work structures (eg, multi-functional teams for routine processes, project teams for one-off assignments), jobs and organisational units. A new 'broad-brush' PSIF was designed and agreed. It contained roughly 50% less staff, operated with four rather than seven levels, and required intensive team-working to be effective. The Prison Board accepted the proposal.

In the second phase, teams of specialist PSIF staff analysed existing processes in detail and redesigned these for maximum simplicity and length of responsibility for team members involved. Pro forma processes were agreed and prepared for 'debugging' later by staff who would operate them. Each of the 200 staff in the division was assessed for suitability for the new process-driven roles, and then either offered a new role or helped to find employment in another government department. Intensive work was undertaken with the IT department to ensure that the new systems and hardware planned for the PSIF would facilitate the new organisation's work. All selected staff were provided with between two and three weeks training, in team-working, process refinement and selected technical skills.

In early February, the 'switch-over' to the new organisation took place. Every PSIF staff member took on a substantially changed role in a radically different organisation. Customers were introduced to new Service Managers whose role was to customise support to each of them and ensure that their needs were met, on time and to specification, with important gaps and issues being identified as customers took on greater accountability for operating work in their establishments and learned to become better customers of PSIF. The new PSIF is approximately 40% less expensive to run and is expecting to achieve even greater efficiencies when the programme of IT change is complete in 1996.

Some key challenges remain within PSIF. The quality of team-working, while significantly higher than before the programme of change, remains patchy and constrained by the grade structures and career progression processes of the civil service in the UK. Work is also required in improving the flexibility in the allocation of resources within PSIF, to cope with varying workloads in different areas. Relations with customers, while also greatly improved, need to become more business-like in many cases, with more stringent and clear measures of performance and satisfaction.

10

PROCESS REDESIGN Q & A

— ◇ —

Q. WHAT IS A PROCESS?

What is a *process*? To paraphrase St Augustine, I would say that I know what it is, but ask me to describe it and I won't find the words. Process is a vague word which encompasses so many meanings that it is hard to pin down. We talk of processing data, of process consultation, of business processes, and so forth, but what do we exactly mean by process? I once heard an eco-biologist describing extinction as a process, not an event. In one formula he had captured something essential both about extinction and processes: processes can be opposed to events. An event happens at one given time. A process keeps happening. We can only capture a process through the events we witness which derive from the process.

Because time is of the essence in processes, they are very difficult to grasp intellectually. All we can have is a series of time-bound pictures, and we usually find it difficult to think dynamically. Furthermore, not all sequences of events are processes. To count as a process, the sequence needs to have an element of causality. For instance, the number of cars which drive in front of your house is a sequence, not a process. Yet, as rush hour approaches, the very number of cars on the roads influences how fast they can drive, which in turn diminishes the number of cars which drive in front of your house at a given time. The sequence becomes a process because an element of causal dependence appears. In light traffic, car A will drive in front of your house independently of what the other cars are doing. Yet, at rush hour, car A can only drive in front of the house if the preceding car, X, has gone by. A's driving past then becomes dependent of another event of the sequence: X's driving past. For our purposes, this is how we will define the notion of process:

> A process is a sequence of dependent events.

In our business context most of the events will be actions. Yet, sometimes, passive effects can trigger further action, so we might as well consider events in general. The three key concepts we are going to focus on to understand how processes work are: dependence, variability and interfaces.

Dependence

Dependence is at the heart of any process. Dependence means that in a sequential process action A needs to be finished before B can be started. In practical terms, the lock needs to be turned before the door can be opened. If the door is still locked, it simply won't open. In sequential processes we find both *necessary* dependencies, and *convenience* dependencies.

> The practical consequence of the dependency principle is that any process is only as efficient as its most inefficient part, as a chain is only as strong as its weakest link. In other terms this means that the most important factor at any given time is the most limiting one.

Variability

Variability is about the normal statistical fluctuations one finds at any step in any process. In itself, it is not always a problem, but when linked to dependence, it can create some serious hassles. Statistical variability accumulates its effects at the end point of the process, in other words, at the finished product end.

> 'Innocent' looking variability at each individual step can create major problems at the end of the process where it 'all comes together'. Furthermore, variability tends to disconnect the location of cause and effect, since a problem upstream will only show as such downstream.

Interfaces

Interfaces are another key element of process theory, yet they are largely ignored. Because of the ways our minds work, we focus on where work actually happens (ie, someone does something). However, many problems deriving from dependence and variability can be found at the interfaces. What is the point of having an excellent operation design if the supplies are continually late or mixed up?

> Interfaces always need to be considered, whether specific as with a production line and its supplies, or more general such as man/machine or design/manufacturing interfaces. Interfaces are where

'natural' dependence breaks in our mind—yet a real dependence still exists.

OVERALL EFFICIENCY AND LOCAL EFFICIENCY

One of the practical implications of the dependence principle has to do with the gap between local efficiency and global efficiency. Let us consider a sequential process of four steps: selling, packaging, shipping and billing. Let us assume that this particular flow hasn't been redesigned and that you need the order to package the goods, then you need the package to ship it and you also need the shipping manifest to bill the client:

We naturally assume that if each step of the process is optimised, the entire process will be equally optimised. This, however, is not quite correct. In most cases, if we optimise each step, we will find that they will process work at *different speeds*. An optimised selling step (we hire Rex Harrison, king of salesmen) can produce five orders per day. Packaging, however, is a bit tricky and can only happen with complex and delicate procedures. With the best equipment in the world, we can package about three orders a day. Once they've been properly packaged, shipping is no problem. With our new super-duper crates, we could easily ship ten orders per day. Unfortunately, billing has always been a bit of a sore point. We are working on it, but because of the complex account structure required to sell our five orders per day, we can only do the invoices for four shipments a day. So, suppose that we start with a blank page, this is what happens at the end of day 1:

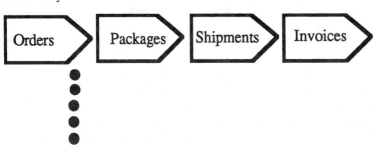

On day 2, three of these orders are carefully packaged, and passed on to shipping. However, Rex is on a roll and he has sold five more items.

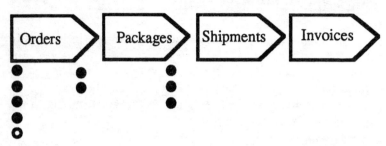

On day 3, the three packaged orders are quite happily shipped, and three more orders packaged. Don't forget that Rex is still selling!

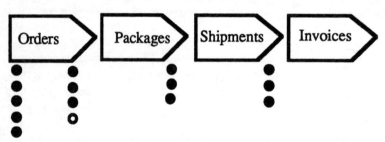

Finally, on day 4 we can bill the client and hopefully get some just returns for our labours.

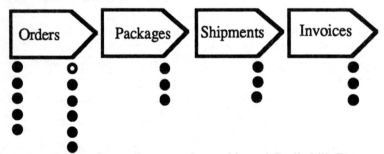

And on it goes, Rex sells, we package, ship and finally bill. But guess what, some of our clients are getting fairly impatient. Check the guy up there who passed a white order in day 2. He desperately needs this shipment. Actually, Rex had promised him that the shipment would be at his plant the next day. When he calls, he is told that his order has not even been processed to packaging. Now he is really irate. He probably tells everyone how badly we let him down. And he is the first of many. Looking at the backlog of orders, we will have to ask Rex to slow down on the selling bit. We simply can't cope. Rex is not very pleased, he is the King of Salesmen. He works on straight commission, why should he slow down? We've got the stuff haven't we, so why can't we get it to the customers? The people out there are ready to buy! Maybe we could speed up a bit this packaging thing, take a few more risks.

As this example shows, optimising each step of the process does not optimise the process as long as the steps run at different speeds. Rex *is* the best, but he will probably end up bringing the company down. Furthermore, all those orders have probably been manufactured or bought before being packaged. However, we will only get paid after we send an invoice. The stock of products which accumulate may count as assets on the balance sheet, but as long as they are not out of the gates and their invoice on the client's desk, we have no cash coming in: we have spent money and hard work and haven't got anything to show for it yet.

It is important to realise that this situation is created by the dependence between the steps in the process. If the steps were independent, none of this would happen. Because of this dependence, the entire system is only as good as its slowest link. If we keep our nose down and only focus on each local step we will never even see the *real* problem we are having. Rex will probably find work elsewhere. After all, he is the King of Salesmen.

Q. WHERE ARE YOUR BOTTLENECKS?

In the preceding example, the packaging step was our bottleneck. This is the slowest link where the workflow slows down hopelessly. Bottlenecks are usually quite easy to spot. In factories, one sees a huge pile of work-in-progress; crates piling up before this or that workstation. In offices, one can easily spot a team of totally harassed-looking individuals who everybody keeps running after because they haven't yet delivered what they had promised by last Friday. Bottlenecks are the key point of the process because they determine its ultimate efficiency. Yet, many managers in charge of processes both in plants and offices wouldn't be able to answer the question:

Q. Could you show me your main bottlenecks?

For that matter, can you? Bottlenecks are not a bad thing in absolute terms. There is no point in 'getting rid of all bottlenecks' simply because getting rid of one fatally creates another somewhere else— remember, the bottleneck is simply the slowest link of the process, regardless of what it does. Yet many bottlenecks can be eased by giving them sufficient attention. Machines can be kept running full time as opposed to the usual 75 per cent. Teams can be expanded or reorganised. The point is not to get rid of one bottleneck, but to get most steps in the process to work roughly to the same rhythm. Remember that in our example, the shipping step was unnecessarily efficient.

Practical Tip: Once you have spotted your main bottleneck, do what you can to ease it. Then use it as a reference point for the desired speed of the other steps.

In a large British sales organisation, one small team of data analysts seemed to be a constant problem. Their internal customers were always complaining that team members looked haggard and were constantly rushed off their feet. The entire organisation seemed to disapprove of these people. At some point, the Finance department redesigned one of its processes. It appeared that this analysis team was a bottleneck very early on in the process because they had to extract financial information from the organisation's IT systems.

When focusing on it, the redesign team realised that many sales managers depended heavily on the same team because they calculated their targets—which were linked to their bonuses. What is more, a few top managers had privileged relationships with some members of the team—who had been there for a long time, but had never climbed the corporate ladder—and would occasionally demand *ad hoc* analysis to support strategic decisions. In effect, the team was felt to be 'useless' by the rest of the organisation because they were a multiple bottleneck: the only people to be able to both extract data from the systems and conduct numerical analyses. No matter how hard these people tried, they would never succeed.

EXPENSIVE EQUIPMENT

The instinctive answer to the bottleneck issue is the 'bigger faster machine'. The reasoning makes sense, if the machine is faster, then things will get better. Unfortunately, we also have a natural tendency to maximise the use of expensive or heavy equipment. In this way we can sometimes create unnecessary dependency on the basis that the equipment is 'very efficient'. What happens is that we direct several processes through that piece of equipment—whether computer or machine tool—because it is so efficient, and because it is so expensive, it needs to 'pay for itself'. The upshot of this is that we create queues where there were none, and instead of relieving the bottleneck we can inadvertently make the problem worse.

As a rule, automation results in a loss of flexibility: an automated system will set its speed of processing. On a perfectly flexible process, one would want to adapt to demand by spreading dependency amongst different numbers of persons, ie 10 for 100 jobs, 1 for 10 jobs. An automated link might add constraints to such flexibility, and create fluctuations.

CASE STUDY: STEELWORKS LTD

Never underestimate the complexity of integrated systems. In some cases, the elimination of 'obvious' bottlenecks only serves to move the problem elsewhere. John McLuckie and Mark Heffernan, founders of the Australian consultancy International Systems Dynamics (ISD), recount their experience in fine-tuning a major integrated steelworks plant in Australia.

Steelworks Ltd operates a fully integrated iron and steel plant on the southern coast of New South Wales (Australia). The plant incorporates four blast furnaces, two basic oxygen steel-making furnaces and a continuous slab-casting plant. The plant has a capacity of approximately 4.5 million tonnes per annum.

Molten iron flows from the blast furnace, is transported in ladles through the system, converted to molten steel and cast into solid slabs of various dimensions. The system was designed to operate on a 'pull through' basis, that is each downstream element was sized to be of greater capacity than the upstream elements, thereby supposedly eliminating bottlenecks.

The only 'escape' valve in the system is to dump surplus molten iron. This results in substantial environmental problems on top of the obvious financial loss. Based on the design capacities of the individual elements this should not happen regularly. However, at the time of ISD's involvement, Steelworks Ltd was regularly dumping 10,000–30,000 tonnes of molten iron per month with corresponding losses in slab production. Steelworks Ltd instigated a 'slab supply improvement program' aimed at minimising the quantity of iron dumped and at improving the reliability of the system in achieving planned outputs of approximately 370,00 tonnes per month. ISD became involved to help the plant in achieving this goal—which was subsequently reached.

The operations were redesigned without major capital investment. ISD consultants worked with a cross-functional team involving internal operations, maintenance, and management personnel. They used the principles of systems dynamics to make explicit the interactions of the various elements within the system and to develop a simulation model (with IThink software). In this case, the simulation process highlighted many shortcomings in the collective knowledge of how the system functioned, and greatly benefited organisational learning.

The model, once completed, represented the capacities, constraints, cycle times, operating rules and philosophies in vogue at the time.

The simulations revealed several key leverage points, such as:

1. The operation of the slab casters at a rate significantly higher than the upstream system capacity resulted in the system being starved of product. This in turn created periods of reduced production and an average production rate less than that which could be achieved by not operating the slab casters at full capacity.

2. The different travel times from the various blast furnaces to the BOS furnaces, and the rules under which torpedo ladles were despatched by rail transport from the blast furnaces resulted in an arrival pattern of molten iron that varied from 0 to 2000 tonnes per hour. This resulted in seemingly minor items of plant being idle or under-utilised for significant periods of time, followed by them being bottlenecks.

Changes to the operating rules and to the scheduling of production were implemented and trialed on the basis of the systems dynamics simulation. This has ultimately resulted in the plant reliably achieving increased production rates of steel slab by an average of 20,000 to 30,000 tonnes per month. Dumping of molten iron no longer occurs on a regular basis.

Q. WHAT IS THE IMPACT OF VARIABILITY?

Statistical fluctuations are often the most 'abstract' concept to handle. No matter how many Statistical Control seminars we have been pushed through, the practical relevance of it can easily seem trivial. However, linked to dependence, statistical fluctuations can mean many very confusing effects. Let us think back to our four step process of selling, packaging, shipping and billing. At the moment we have the following situation:

Day	Orders	Packaged	Shipped	Billed
1	5			
2	7	3		
3	9	3	3	
4	11	3	3	3
5	13	3	3	3

Let us suppose that Rex, the King of Salesmen, regularly sells five per day. Yet our packaging process, which is so delicate, isn't as regular. On some days we can actually package five, but on others we cannot do better than two. This is what would happen:

Day	Orders	Packaged	Shipped	Billed
1	5			
2	6	4		
3	9	2	4	
4	11	3	2	4
5	11	5	3	2

Rex's over-performance is not as obvious. Sure, the backlog grows, but not that fast. Furthermore, we understand why we could only package two when the packaging machine broke down, but using our sophisticated shipping system for just two items is ridiculous. It is simply not cost efficient. What we really should do when this happens is subcontract the shipping to someone else. So, for two days a week we use our vast shipping capacity for something else.

Day	Selling	Packaging	Shipping	Billing
1	5			
2	6	4		
3	9	2	4	
4	11	3	2	0
5	11	5	5	4

What happens is that now, by making a very reasonable decision, suddenly the billing department cannot cope. On day 4 the manager throws a fit because his accountants are sitting around doing nothing, and the next day, all of a sudden, out of the blue, they have to do five. Hang on a second, four is the utmost limit: this is absolutely intolerable.

As we fiddle the system to make it more cost efficient, we create further dependency by adding another process to the same step: shipping. As we do that, with the normal variability of each of the steps we also blur any logical cause-effect relationship we could have previously spotted. Furthermore, the billing department, under pressure from its manager who is not happy to see her staff doing nothing, starts 'getting ahead' with another task. In effect it is creating more work-in-progress. This new work will have to be dealt with in some fashion by the organisation, and so forth. Fundamentally, the combination of variability and dependence will push managers to make decisions which will worsen the overall situation—not make it better. After a while the process becomes not only totally impossible to manage, but also incomprehensible as each new decision over-compensates for the previous one.

VARIABILITY ACCUMULATES THROUGH A DEPENDENT SYSTEM

Accidents happen when variability accumulates at the wrong point. Suppose that in our process all elements are variable, not by much, but Rex sells six one day, four the next and six the next, and the same happens at each step. We could very well end up with this situation:

Day	Orders	Packaged	Shipped	Billed
1	6			
2	10	2		
3	12	2	2	
4	13	4	0	2
5	13	4	4	0

Any shopkeeper will tell you that some days no one comes into the shop, yet other days, customers keep walking in, to the point that you can't serve them all. This variability is difficult enough to handle at a shop level, but if we have an entire process behind the shop, it gets worse. Typically, one part of the process is overloaded whilst the rest has nothing to do. This shouldn't be a problem in itself, but most of the time, the departments with nothing to do over-correct by finding some work to be done, which then comes in the way of the original work being slowly processed by the bottleneck. It is exactly the kind of bad luck which can bring a company down. Customers can be dissatisfied enough to cancel orders, whilst at the same time the cash flow is negative for long enough to hurt. What happens is that companies will create security stocks at each point of the process to protect themselves from this insane situation. These stocks in turn add more confusion and variability to the system because they give more opportunity for over-compensation.

Unfortunately, minor acceptable local variations can accumulate to stress the end-of-process point—often, the product. At the end of the day many 'minor' problems can result in customer dissatisfaction. Each inspection point might well be passed, but it is hard to predict how many such variations could combine by the end of the process. What is certain is that every process has the same end point: its customer.

Q. ARE YOU AWARE OF INTERFACES?

Finally, interfaces are the most commonly ignored part of any process, most likely because they often fit with 'territory' boundaries. However, they are a critical part of any process because they tend to hide 'invisible' dependencies. Two different processes can have very strong functional links, and still be considered separate because of the way the organisational chart is drawn up. In effect, this critical dependency will become invisible to all, and a constant source of problems. Typically, the two teams in charge will be in constant relation—either positively or negatively. In lean manufacturing, the greatest area of interface where traditional functional chimneys have obscured dependency can be found in the design/manufacture area. Traditionally, engineers would design products and then pass on the plans to manufacturing, who would then have to construct the proper tools and methods for construction. However, what makes sense from a design point of view is not necessarily easy to manufacture. The dependency is very strong because, basically, nothing can be manufactured until it has been designed. Many firms are now trying to integrate product design and production design into one department to make that dependence explicit.

WATCH OUT FOR FEEDING PROCESSES

Because of the general complexity and diversity of operations, one focuses on one's area of expertise. Unfortunately, the most limiting factor might be found elsewhere. As opposed to actual operations, the supply side of component parts can hide many problems. An operator might spend five full seconds wiggling a component out of the supply heap, and then a few milliseconds placing it. In the same way, an analyst might spend half a day doing a rather complex financial analysis, having spent a week getting all the information together from various internal sources.

Q. DO YOU CONTROL FEEDBACK EFFECTS?

Feedback is a particular form of dependency. In essence feedback is self-dependency in a process: a task is dependent on the outcome of another task further down the line from it. For instance, selling is often dependent on the amount of cash generated by previous sales. More cash, more selling and advertising—hence more sales. Less cash, less money available for selling actions, and in all likelihood less sales.

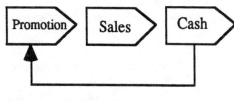

Feed-back loop

Amplifying effect

This is the vicious or virtuous circle, when two elements mutually reinforce each other: when A increases, B increases, and when A decreases, B decreases—as in Sales increases Cash, which increases Promotion and, in turn, Sales. This structure generates runaway effects, or in other terms, exponential growth or decay:

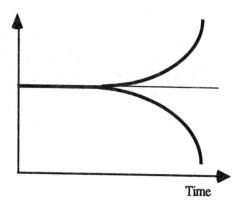

Time

Balancing effect

If A has a positive influence on B (if A increases, B increases and if

A decreases, B decreases), but B has a negative influence on A (if B increases, the A decreases and if B decreases, then A increases), this is a goal-seeking loop, or balancing process. Any external action by B will be followed by a return to its stable position:

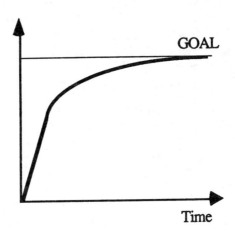

Oscillations

If a dominant negative feedback loop has a delay built in, meaning that the influence of A over B will be delayed by a certain time-lapse, the system will oscillate until it returns to its original position.

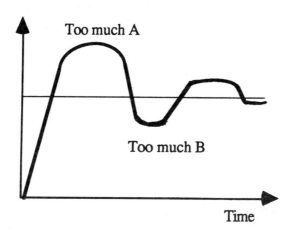

THE FORRESTER EFFECT

A conjunction of variability and feedback can have quite drastic effects on a business process. Jay Forrester[14] first identified this problem in a distribution chain. He showed how small market variations could create major overshoots at the production stage because of delays in feedback. Let us consider the following situation.

Your firm sells widgets which are produced, then stocked at a dispatching warehouse before being sold to a wholesaler, who will then sell to retailers:

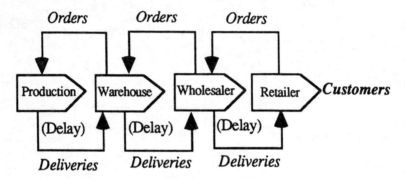

Once a week, your wholesaler sends his truck to deliver the week's order to the retailer. The retailer then fills in a form saying how many widgets she wants delivered next week. From all these forms, the wholesaler sends you an order, which you dispatch from the warehouse. Your production people calculate how much to produce from what the warehouse tells them.

In normal circumstances, the retailer sells about one widget a day. Suppose the retailer keeps zero stock (the widgets are expensive). On Saturday, you will deliver five widgets for next week. The retailer's inventory will look like this:

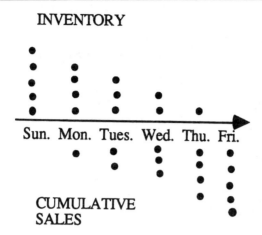

Your Marketing Department decides to run a massive Widget advertising campaign. Nobody bothers to warn the retailer since the wholesaler knows all about it. The campaign is amazingly successful and twice as many people start buying widgets. Consequently, the retailer now sells two widgets a day.

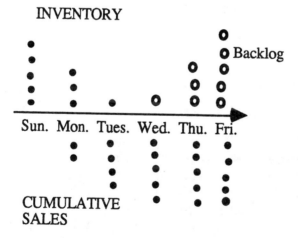

By Wednesday, she has run out of widgets to sell! By Friday, she has already promised five customers that she will get the widgets for them next week at all costs. They were disgruntled, but sufficiently convinced by the commercials to wait until Monday to buy their widgets. On Saturday, when the delivery truck arrives, the retailer realises with shock and horror that he has only brought the five widgets ordered last week! Supposing she sells those five she has promised on Monday, she will be out of widgets for the entire week. And what if people continue to buy like crazy? She makes a swift mental calculation and decides she needs at least ten widgets delivered on Monday to cover the week!

However, when she phones the wholesaler, she hears that all other retailers have been ordering like crazy. The best they can do is send her an extra delivery of five on Monday which should cover her for the week. She is furious, she tells the wholesaler she is actually losing sales because of their incompetence. If all she gets is five extra widgets on Monday, then she needs 15 more for her Saturday delivery: five to service customers, and ten as a stock for next week.

At the wholesaler's everyone is going crazy. The ten retailers are all phoning in for extra deliveries for Monday, and placing increased orders. Instead of a change of order from five to ten as they had anticipated, the retailers are ordering an average of 15 widgets for next week. With ten retailers, the order is of 150 widgets, whereas the warehouse is only scheduled to deliver 100!

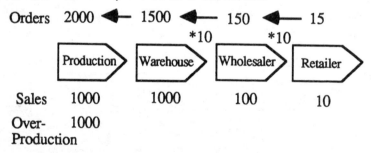

Because they anticipate the delay in the delivery—they won't get what they need when they need it—the retailers are over-compensating in their orders to the wholesaler. The wholesalers who have just been cut short are likely to do the same. Remember that as the orders come in to the wholesaler, the warehouse is only delivering the scheduled increase of 100 instead of 150. The wholesalers do not have enough widgets to deliver the 15 asked by their retailers. Eventually, the warehouse will ask Production to come up immediately with the missing widgets.

Unfortunately, this increase in orders does not correspond to the actual increase in sales. Sure, sales have doubled—from five to ten—for each retailer. But not tripled! In a few weeks, the retailers will find themselves with a stock they do not need and send it back to the wholesaler, who will in turn send it back to the warehouse, and so forth. With this simple example, we can see how variations can ripple through a system and be amplified at each stage because of the delay in the response of each of the elements. Each step in the process anticipates and over-corrects, creating havoc upstream.

THE MOST LIMITING FACTOR

In a more general sense, the most critical factor *at any given time* is the most limiting one. The difficulty is that this most limiting factor is not necessarily obvious. For instance, it is rarely the largest one. When baking bread, at some point you will have to add a bit of yeast to the flour. No amount of additional flour will make the bread rise. The trouble with the *most limiting factor* is that, in many cases, it is not obvious to the eye. Some key competence that staff miss; some scarce resource which is taken for granted, and so on. The problem is accrued by the fact that the most limiting factor changes with time. Just as with bottlenecks, the moment you have cracked one problem then another one becomes the most limiting—even if not quite yet.

There is no predicting the next limiting factor. Some 'known' indicators of disaster such as world population growth or the American budget deficit can be either insignificant or crippling to our economies in future years. There is no way of knowing. The only answer is to keep an operational perspective and to look for factors, often taken for granted, which would make the whole thing grind to a halt if they disappeared. Then check the available supply of these things. If the supply is low, worry.

Many firms were caught unawares with the end of the recession. Understandably, the firms that rode the recession well were those able to ruthlessly keep their headcount down. Yet, as the economy picked up again, ever so slightly, those very firms suddenly ran into endless problems because they could not respond to the increase in orders. Many then relied massively on temps, without either training or motivation, and had a rash of quality problems as a result. In effect, nothing fails like success, and one solution simply moves the most limiting factor to another area.

Q.DOES RE-ENGINEERING NECESSARILY MEAN REDUNDANCY?

The answer is 'No'! Re-engineering does not necessarily imply re-dundancy. It is, however, an important question to address because most people will expect to see some link. Up to now, we have focused mainly on technical questions about understanding how processes work. I believe that without a deep understanding of what a process is and how it works, managers are unlikely to achieve any substantial success in their re-engineering efforts. However, the 'human' dimension must not be underestimated. In most re-engineering pro-grammes staff share the suspicion that all the effort is nothing more than a cover-up for a massive redundancy programme. In many respects, these suspicions can be understood because:

- Redesign necessarily means fundamental changes in the organisa-tion of work, and some jobs are bound to disappear or be significantly modified.
- Some companies have used re-engineering as a cover-up for laying-off staff.
- At an individual level any change is highly stressful and creates anxiety about one's place in the new set-up.

This is all the more true as the very aim of re-engineering is simpli-fication of processes for increased productivity. Increased productiv-ity can easily be understood as less people to do the same amount of work. Of course, this is a typical case of the 'fixed pie' mentality we try to change with redesign workshops. Increased productivity means more people freed to do value added work.

RE-ENGINEERING DOESN'T MEAN REDUNDANCY, BUT MOBILITY

Re-engineering, however, does mean change. As we move from local to global projects, more than one process is redesigned, lead-time is reduced, and a new dynamic motivation appears in the company. And with it, the question of what to do with this new impetus appears. Obviously, if we redesign all processes down to 50 per cent lead-time, at least 25 per cent staff become redundant in theory. What are we to do with this slack? The short-term view is often to get rid of them.

This, it turns out, is both misguided and dangerous. Considering the pace of change in markets, a company which is simply more efficient at doing what it always did is no less vulnerable. The key issue is how to use excess staff to develop new product or service lines in order to stay 'one-step ahead' of the market!

Corporate flexibility: competing processes

Why would extremely successful companies such as Toyota still worry about improving production line operations? Why still try to minimise the number of staff necessary to run one line? The insight is both profound and obvious: a product line is short lived. In two years, the product becomes obsolete and something new has to be introduced on the market. How does this work internally? The old product can't simply be stopped—it needs to be phased out. Meanwhile, production of the new product needs to increase as sales are pushed.

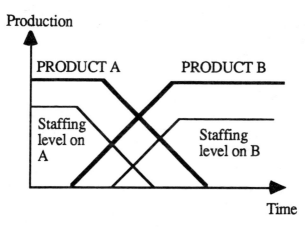

For this to work, one needs to have both:

■ Flexible production lines: 10 people on the line to respond to a demand of 100 products, but only one person on the line if the demand is for only 10 products.
■ Flexible staff which can operate all the jobs on the line. If the demand is high, each person will do one job repetitively, whereas if the the demand is low, one person will do all the jobs from start to finished product.

In such a set-up, processes are competing internally all the time. Process redesign is absolutely essential to free up resources to create a new competitive process. There is no question of redundancy since the firm which can master this dynamic will be expanding overall. Yet, a single process would still need to be reduced and ultimately disbanded to support the newer, growing ones.

Equating re-engineering with redundancy is a clear proof of terminal short-sightedness. Re-engineering is necessary for expansion. It is by freeing up *experienced* internal resources that new, competitive offerings can be brought to the market.

Staff flexibility

Such a dynamic also relies on staff flexibility. Process operators must be both willing and able to move from one job to the next. As anyone who has been involved in a change project will know, convincing someone to move is the trickiest thing in the world. Most likely, people will accept if it means a move up the hierarchy, which is exactly what we want to avoid—since such development would soon create the endless hierarchical ladder.

The two fundamental issues we deal with are:

- *Competency*: in practice, this means training to be able to move from one set of tasks to another.
- *Motivation*: what incentives are we going to propose to individuals so that they are willing to move? This can often be dealt with on an individual basis rather than as a company-wide policy since each person will have a different set of needs.

To keep abreast of the human resources problems that a total re-engineering will cause, we can build the following matrix:

Name	Present job	New job	Training needs	Incentives	Flexibili
John	job description in terms of task responsibility	tasks in new position	specific training needs	What interests John? Why would he want to move?	What capabilit to move h he demonstr ed in the past?
Mary					
Sue					

From productivity to market share

Another way to exploit increase in productivity is by immediate pressure on price. In many markets, customers are actually more price sensitive than one might think. This is particularly true in terms of the shift of power towards consumers: it's a buyer's market. In these circumstances, if management has the courage to pass on the savings immediately to the customers, the chances are that a productivity increase transferred to a price decrease will soon (6 months) generate an increased market share. The company which would have used the productivity gains to dismiss staff would then find itself dramatically understaffed to deal with the demand increase, and would need to hire new, inexperienced workers—or worse, re-hire the people it has just laid-off!

BE UP-FRONT ABOUT YOUR INTENTIONS

Senior managers often dismiss what staff think, or how they feel about things. This is understandable considering how little contact they have with workplace level operators—yet it is still hard to understand. Workplace operators are those who actually make the product, provide the service, and constitute the organisation. It is their work that management is supposed to organise. Unless one has witnessed the effects of a mismanaged change project at shop-floor level, one can hardly imagine how organisations can literally grind to a halt. Staff need some sort of understanding about *what to expect* if they are to get on with their work. If not, they'll spend more time trying to find out what is going on than actually achieving anything as regards to work or change. Anxiety and uncertainty bring out the worst in everybody, and when this happens collectively, the resulting environment can be downright ugly.

Practical Tip: Be up-front about your intentions. If you don't intend to lay-off staff say so. If a redundancy programme is on the cards, announce it and go through with it as fast as you can. Whatever you do, don't keep workplace staff guessing.

The large company dilemma

Large, old companies can get caught in unpleasant dynamics. Firms such as merchant banks or steelworks are often very dependent on the business environment. With a few points change in interest rates or commodity prices they can suddenly swing from making millions in profit to showing millions in losses. In the down-turns, such firms tend to lay-off staff (which usually accounts for very little of the actual loss) as an appeasing measure to shareholders. Top management can then be seen as 'doing something'. Most of the times such programmes are labelled as 'downsizing' or 'restructuring', but in a few unfortunate cases, they are also called 're-engineering'. Precious little re-engineering often happens in such cases, but it is necessary to understand that such things happen, and staff will hear about them because they are usually very well publicised.

Listen to Machiavelli

Machiavelli once advised that *if you are going to do good, do it little by little, if you are about to do evil, do it all at once.* This certainly holds true for redundancy programmes. If it has to happen, slash brutally and suddenly. Remaining staff who have survived the *blitzkrieg* will usually count their blessings, spot the career opportunities opened by the cuts and get back to work with a vengeance. On the other side, if cut-backs are rumoured but never materialise, all sorts of negative dynamics and game-playing overtake the organisation, and actual production of value soon becomes a secondary concern. The worst happens when, in large organisations, units or departments 'disappear' progressively over a length of time. Such a practice—which can make some managerial sense as in 'cutting out the dead wood'—creates a paranoid working environment in which resistance to change will achieve new heights and very little work will get done.

MANAGE MOODS

If embarked upon a genuine full-scale re-engineering programme, you will have to manage the organisation's mood. The challenge is of course to get involvement from staff. It must be understood that this involvement varies greatly over time and is very dependent both on expectations and 'proof' of management delivery. It can be sometimes surprising to find out what staff consider to be proof, either of management commitment or duplicity, but it must none the less be taken very seriously!

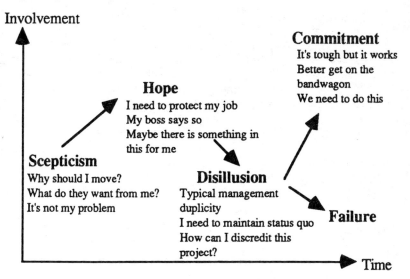

Involvement

Commitment
It's tough but it works
Better get on the bandwagon
We need to do this

Hope
I need to protect my job
My boss says so
Maybe there is something in this for me

Scepticism
Why should I move?
What do they want from me?
It's not my problem

Disillusion
Typical management duplicity
I need to maintain status quo
How can I discredit this project?

Failure

Time

Limit rumours

In practice, try to limit rumours by a clear and effective information policy. Many projects actually set up communication procedures but fail to respect them, mostly through missing announcement deadlines. The only way to reassure staff is to be rigorous about the announced deadlines and to be consistent in what you say.

Remember, in change projects, benefit of the doubt is rarely given to management. The onus is on management to prove that they are reliable and know what they are doing.

Don't humiliate staff

At all costs, avoid humiliating staff. This can happen easily.

A large sales organisation going through a major re-engineering effort set-up a 'cost control' project. The idea was both 'empowered' and simple. Each department had to come up with a suggestion on how to reduce costs as a measure of commitment to the change effort. The upshot of it was that departments found little things here and there that they could cut. Typically this meant no tea and cookies, reduced staff privileges in terms of memberships to local health-clubs, reduction of the company car policy, travelling expenses, and so forth. In total, this amounted to reductions which barely covered 5% of the consulting cost for the re-engineering project. Yet, each of these measures had a significant impact on people's practical lives. The result was a deep feeling of resentment and powerlessness which did much to slow down the project and disqualify its legitimacy.

Such incidents can happen easily from lack of concern or forethought, but their damage impact is rarely taken seriously by management. In any full-scale change project, one needs to remain aware that appreciation varies considerably from one management level to the next.

CASE STUDY: ALULADDER CORP

Renault Quality Institute consultant Michel Marissal managed the re-engineering of the production plant of a French aluminium ladder manufacturer. AluLadder Corp is a small company with a complement of about 200 people. They are specialised in ladders, mostly aluminium, but with some special orders in fibre or steel components. The plant had six workshops each with independent workstations. Each workstation would release piles of half-finished ladders (about 20). So many ladders were stocked around the workstations that people could not even see one another. Each operator had a production bill to fill in, which was subsequently treated by a complex production scheduling system. In the best case, a product going from entry (materials) to exit (finished products) would take two and a half days.

By organising a pull system the redesign team re-organised the entire plant on a Just-in-Time basis, and minimised work-in-progress ladders which previously could be found at each stage of production. The team used basic re-engineering principles such as parallel processing and upstream-downstream organisation to streamline production. In practice, three 5-day workshops were organised with consultants and local staff, and practical solutions were directly implemented to apply these general principles. The initial workshops were followed up six months later by further work, led, this time, by the previous workshop leaders as opposed to consultants. Fine-tuning followed six months later in a 3-day final workshop. At the outset of the process, lead-time had come down from two and a half days to two hours from start to finish per ladder.

In effect, by the end of the year, the plant had increased productivity by 30% and in the meantime generated 45% excess capacity! The immediate reaction was to reduce staff to meet current capacity requirements, but top management took the time to consider the implications of the plant redesign. First, they rethought the very nature of their investment. Whereas beforehand they had thought of investment in terms of heavy equipment (to cope with all cases) they realised that investment needed to be light and flexible, which could work in the Just-in-Time system. Furthermore, at the same time, many hyper-markets were getting into ladder sales and needed to work with low costs. They expected very fast response from suppliers, as well as below market prices. AluLadder was suddenly able to respond to these customers' requirements, holding low stocks both in the hyper-markets and their own plant.

This made them leader in the French market, and also pushed them forward on the German market. In these circumstances, their extra capacity enabled them to respond to a demand that sky-rocketed. Had they accepted the 'common' wisdom about capacity, they would have downsized staff, only to be cut short by the rapid increase in demand. In AluLadder's case, the tremendous pace of events—from redesign to increased demand—saved them from having to consider hard choices for too long. Six months later, they were recruiting further.

Q. WHAT ABOUT TECHNOLOGY?

You may have noticed that I haven't given much attention to Information Technology (IT) as a redesign panacea. This can surprise many who are used to hearing about re-engineering and IT as two sides of the same coin. The confusion between the re-engineering area and IT 'magical solutions' has come about for a number of reasons, such as:

■ The first people to seriously talk and write about re-engineering were mostly from IT.

■ The media tend to focus on spectacular improvements with a 'great big computer' at the centre of things—it introduces a number of 'angles' to otherwise technical and boring organisational issues.

■ It is often easier to buy the packaged IT solution than to actually change the way we organise our work.

This last reason in particular has created much heartache in companies, and led to recent reassessments of IT's value for money. The point is that if you computerise an organisational mess, all you get is a computerised mess. The chances are that it won't show as much, but it will still be as inefficient—although the problems may often be shifted somewhere else in the organisation. There is no doubt that IT has penetrated our organisations to an extraordinary extent, and that it has required an ever-growing share of our budgets. Yet, what are the overall yields? In the foreword of a major MIT study on the impact of IT on business, Lester Thurow[15] observes:

> Specific cases in which the new technologies have permitted huge increase in output or decreases in costs can be cited, but when it comes to the bottom line there is no clear evidence that these new technologies have raised productivity (the ultimate determinant of our standard of living) or profitability. In fact, precisely the opposite is true. There is evidence, in the United States at least, that the investment in the new technologies has coincided with lowered overall productivity and profitability.'

The correlation can, of course, be totally spurious. Yet the doubt itself should be enough to slow down our 'fix it with technology' impulse. In particular in the service sector, which is heavily equipped with IT equipment, productivity is not just levelling out. According to Peter Drucker, it is actually worsening! None the less we often feel that we cannot afford to be less equipped than our competitors. In that respect, we have created a sort of corporate addiction to IT. What advantage can we get out of IT then? Researcher Thomas Davenport suggests that to be of any use to the business, IT has to be linked with process innovation.[16] He argues that we cannot expect an IT investment in itself to provide economic return. Only change in a process can yield productivity benefits, and IT's role is to make a new process design possible.

IT as an enabler—not a solution

This notion of IT as an enabler is a key concept to fit IT within process redesign work. No IT solution in itself can help us do things that old pen-and-paper methods would never allow. Yet, these applications must be seen as specific tools within a workflow pattern. With this in mind, Davenport proposes the following matrix to understand IT benefits.

	IT initiative	*Process change*	*Economic outcome*
Individual	Laptop system	Sales call	Sales
Work Group	Product Database	Product Movement	Product Management
Business Unit	Product Management System	Channel Relationships	Competitive Position

IT works when the firm thinks of deploying IT in conjunction with another key lever, not by itself. When this link is achieved, however, the gains can be spectacular, as the following *BusinessWeek* story illustrates:

Dr James Cimino had a problem. To find out if his patient's confusion was a sign of neurological disease, Cimino needed to test the man's spinal fluid. But scheduling a visit to Columbia Presbyterian Hospital's busy neurology unit was difficult. So he made a note on his computer: Order a spinal tap the next time the patient's chronic heart condition brought him in to the New York City hospital's emergency room. Two weeks later, the patient was there. And yes, having read Cimino's note—which was stored with the patient's records in the hospital's computer system—doctors did the spinal tap.

The case exemplifies how re-engineering hospitals with sophisticated computer networks can help cure one of medicine's worst ills—inefficiency. 'Up to 40% of all hospital costs are related to the generation and storage of information, so it makes sense that information technology can improve efficiency', says Dr William M Tierney of Wishard Memorial Hospital in Indianapolis. Wishard now requires doctors to order all drugs and treatments for patient via computer. The system then automatically warns of potential problems, such as allergic reactions or duplicated tests. Doctors tend to make fewer mistakes. The result: Costs per patient are $900 less.

What can IT do for us?

In any process, IT can help us to achieve substantial results by modifying either the nature of single operations, or the structure of the work flows. IT can do a number of things for us:

Automate

By eliminating human work from a few steps in the process, IT can get rid of a boring job whilst increasing speed and reliability. This will increase productivity on specific segments of the process.

A clever use of automation can be seen in some applications of expert systems. For instance, when a process needs to accommodate (i) trivial cases, (ii) difficult cases and (iii) very complex cases, the trivial cases can be totally delegated to an expert program which 'blindly' processes the information. As Pareto dictates that 80% of cases tend to be trivial, such a system can dramatically improve productivity—simply by not blocking trivial cases in a queue behind more complex ones.

Communication

By creating interactive databases, IT can effectively suppress many time-consuming non value added jobs such as passing documents from one department to another.

> Such systems have been particularly useful in industry. Many manu- facturers are trying to merge their product conception and production design efforts in order to create new 'easy to manufacture' products. This is a nightmare in itself because a vast number of people need to be kept informed of technical changes happening up and down the process stream. A clever distributed database can give access to such information simply by looking up what has been changed in the last period.

Tracking

Keeping track of how well (or badly) we do is necessary for any rigorous approach to business. However, any sort of monitoring tends to be both dull and distracting. It is typically the sort of thing a machine handles very well since it gets neither bored nor distracted.

> Johnson & Johnson, for instance, employs a database at their new centralised research facility which enables executives to track the progress of drugs through the research and development cycle. Know- ing the status throughout the pipeline helps them to avoid bottle- necks—too many drugs entering clinical trials at once—and eliminate drugs which show less promise at particular points in the pipeline.[16]

Simulation and analysis

Obviously, IT can also be used to do weird and wonderful things with the data it provides. Such analyses will help managers to get a better understanding of how markets evolve. Simulations can be very useful to experiment with various alternatives before deciding.

CASE STUDY: PLASTIC INC

If we were a speciality plastic manufacturer, producing various forms of industrial plastic for industrial use, how could we use information technology to improve our operations? We could do a number of things.

Start with the obvious and simplify the billing system. Rather than send an invoice, agree with your long-standing clients that they pay you on receipt of the product. The shipping manifest serves as the invoice. This considerably simplifies the billing process, but needs a robust computer system to link shipments with orders.

We could also provide our salespeople with expert systems on portable computers which would help them to increase sales. For instance, as the salesperson discusses specific product issues with the customer, the system could flag other related products that the firm could also provide for this customer. In a highly technical business where product references go into the thousands, this is more information than even an expert salesperson could store in his or her mind. Furthermore, the database could also relate specific problems to our own in-house experts and help the salesman direct the customer to the right support person.

We could of course redesign our order management system with a clever system which would split the orders in terms of complexity on the one hand, and help channel all enquiries about the various stages of the order to the same case manager who would be a contact point for all enquiries from one client.

If we try to integrate research and development and manufacturing, we could use a network system which would enable engineers based in different geographical locations to communicate easily and be regularly updated on what work has been done that might concern them.

Q. HOW ABOUT PROCESS MODELLING COMPUTER PACKAGES?

Although I prefer working on live issues with pen and paper, I have found several instances where using process modelling computer software can be very useful. This is when the processes are so complex that we can't handle them with simple techniques. When there is no other choice—use the computer.

LEARNING THROUGH SIMULATING

The benefit of computer simulations is to create a learning environment where managers can learn about processes and test possible strategies. In practice, it is often better to have people learn on live issues, but in some cases the risks can be simply too great—or the issue too complex. The simulation is then definitely the next best thing. In his classic article 'Planning as Learning', A de Geus, former head of Shell Group Planning, summarises the impact of computer simulation on the learning process:

> Why not rely on the natural learning process that occurs whenever a management team meets? For us at Shell, there are three compelling reasons. First, although the models in the human mind are complex, most people can deal with only three or four variables at a time and do so through only one or two iterations ...

> The second reason for putting mental models into computers is that in working with dynamic models, people discover that in complex systems (like markets or companies) cause and effect are separated in time and place. To many people such insight is also counter-intuitive. Most of us, particularly if we are engaged in the process of planning, focus on the effect we want to create and then look for the most immediate cause to create that effect. The use of dynamic models helps us discover other trigger points, separated in time and place from the desired effect.

> Lastly, by using computer models we learn what constitutes relevant information. For only when we start playing with these micro-worlds do we find out what information we really need to know.[17]

WHAT PACKAGES?

Until recently, there were few software packages available to support process analysis, simulation or redesign. However, over the past few years, a new generation of specialist software has appeared on the market which focuses primarily on process work. In an exhaustive report on the area from Business Intelligence, Alison Classe presents several applications of these packages:[18]

British Telecom used the Cimulation Centre's Siman and Arena during several process redesign exercises, including a reorganisation of its directory enquiries service. This was achieved by simulating the effect of networking 50 automatic call distribution centres together and ensuring that any consequent changes could be undertaken with fewer risks.

Eagle Star Life first used P-E's Hocus to model processes and conduct simulation for contingency planning. The company's commitment to pay compensation to customers when target service levels are not achieved acted as a driver to ensure that its processes for handling their claims were watertight. The tool helped identify numerous areas where paper flows could be eliminated and where automation could remove the scope for error.

General Motors chose Action Technologies' Toolset to conduct a series of pilot schemes to evaluate the use of process modelling and workflow enabling methods and software. The company wanted tools to support quality improvement and had its own methodology to do so, yet software-based support for the method was lacking. The resulting model facilitates process analysis, using terms which are easily understood, so that improvements can be readily implemented.

Granada UK Rental chose TOP-IX to aid management and process improvement and the redesign of cross-functional processes. Tasks included work and performance measurement and resource planning. The tool's benchmarking ability meant that the company had a firm foundation on which to base its aims for the future, and derived benefits from efficiency measures instead of just cutting costs.

International Research and Development used SFI Advisor as a management aid in the decision-making process, to help identify important activities and prioritise work accordingly. This helped the company to identify key areas within the business after a merger of two disparate cultures, and led to the development of a new 'front-end strategy'. The tool improved the quality of decisions made by assisting managers through the decision-making process.

National & Provincial built its own tool to aid process redesign throughout the company. It bought Virtual Software Factory, a meta-CASE tool, and used it to develop Business Improvement Facility. This tool has begun to address process design and systems development and team design. By using software to automate clerical and statistical aspects in a co-ordinated manner, the process design teams became free to focus on real business issues.

None the less, not all companies surveyed used computerised tools. Whyte and Mackay used a paper-based approach for a major organisational review. The company identified one critical process that it wanted to redesign: the central order fulfilment area of the business. Consequently, it revamped its organisational structure around it. Besides the more radical redesign of a major process, the company also found other opportunities where cost saving simplifications could readily be made.

SYSTEMS DYNAMICS SIMULATIONS

Within the world of computer simulation, the Systems Dynamics subset is particularly interesting for process work since the concept and language was specifically designed to portray dynamic behaviour. The Systems Dynamics framework rests on the following key concepts:

■ *Stocks and Flows*: Stocks and flows are Systems Thinking's two main variables. By manipulating stocks and flows we can draw operational, dynamic representations of how things work. Systems Dynamics can help build computer models of such operations.

■ *Feedback Loops*: constitute the key dynamic element of Systems Thinking. By understanding and using feedback loops we can draw the underlying structures of dynamic behaviour.

■ *Interconnection*: most real-life problems cannot be isolated from their context. The Systems Thinking framework helps us to take into account the complex interconnection of variables which drive behaviour. As such, it is a particularly useful tool to model and simulate dynamic behaviour, particularly as regards feed-back loops and their effects on business events.

CASE STUDY: PROCESS DESIGN AND SYSTEM SIMULATION

The Boston based consultancy Ventana Systems Inc. has developed its own software for dynamic modelling. Bob Eberlein describes how Vensim is used for process redesign.

Most tools that deal with process design are, appropriately, focused very narrowly on the process being designed. Yet, this very focus makes it difficult to address broader issues, such as: Is the right process being redesigned? Will other processes be adversely affected? Does it really matter? In most cases it is not practical to deal with these issues in a meaningful way given the level of detail necessary for process simulation. The main advantage of Vensim system simulation is that it is less detailed and can take on broader issues.

Consider the case of a manufacturer in a cyclical industry re-engineering parts procurement in order to improve productivity and increase output during times of expansion. The original procurement process was based on managerial estimates along with a trigger re-order for parts in stock as shown here:

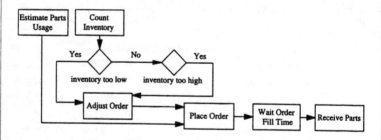

Based on a perception from the floor that there are parts shortages, a new materials planning process is to be put in place. This process takes the form:

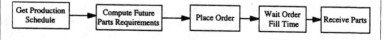

The process has been streamlined, and uses planned production to compensate for the order fill time. The important question that remains is whether this new parts procurement problem will help production meet targets during times of increasing demand. To get a handle on this we use a systems simulation model of the entire production process.

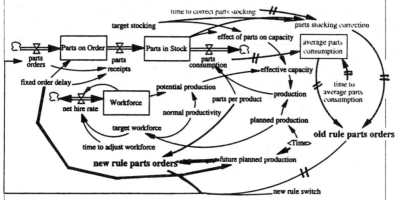

The old process is shown with crossed lines. The new process is shown with thick lines. The results of the new and old process on production relative to planned production can now easily be seen:

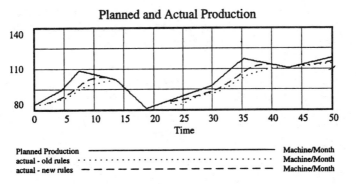

The new process has improved performance, but not as much as might have been hoped or expected. Because of the importance of workforce in the production process, fixing parts supply can only have limited effects.

In addition to helping us see the relative importance of different processes, the Vensim simulation has uncovered a problem with the new parts procurement process. A graph of parts in stock over time shows a continual drift upward.

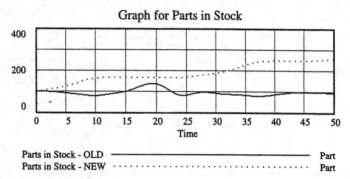

Graph for Parts in Stock

| Parts in Stock - OLD | ————————————— | Part |
| Parts in Stock - NEW | · | Part |

The redesigned process cut the feedback from the actual amount of parts in stock, and this has left a new process that drifts—and will therefore require a further process to be corrected.

This example illustrates the value of such systems simulation as part of the redesign process. The problem, as it turned out, was neither parts procurement nor the number of people, but the relative skill of the workforce. In upturns less skilled people were brought on and took a significant amount of time to achieve the productivity levels of the existing, experienced workers.

CONCLUSION

———— ✦ ————

'God is in the details' once said the architect Mies van der Rohe,[19] and this applies emphatically to organisational design. Organisation is about co-ordinating tasks so that we can process ever-increasing quantities of goods and services. Yet, each specific task has its own impact, which ripples through the system. Because of the increasing diversity and complexity of tasks, we tend to ignore tasks and focus on overall measures such as financial results or organisational structures. And, to tell the truth, this has worked well for years. As long as economic growth was driving the machine, the issue was always to produce faster, not better or cheaper. Now times have changed, and the upper hand is with those who can produce high quality goods at low prices and with fast response—both in terms of customer service and change of offering. To be able to achieve this, there is no other way but to focus again on tasks and how they fit with each other to form operational processes.

In turn, this means mobilising the knowledge and experience *of the people on the job*. Serious re-engineering will not happen in management meeting rooms, but in the workplace—on the open plan or on the shop-floor. Certainly, for the improvements to become permanent, management must change some fundamental policies, but policies in themselves will not affect the practical nature of work. Restructuring the company to be more 'customer focused', moving managers around, downsizing, outsourcing and so on will change traditional management indicators such as functions, roles, and budgets, but will not affect the reality of work in the slightest. No matter how much you restructure the top layer of the company, the same tasks will still need to be done for the product or the service to be delivered to the customer at the end of the day. And, as we have learned from agriculture and production, it is at work level that the productivity issue makes a difference. So how will we apply these advances to the wider realm of 'organisation'?

To make re-engineering lessons work in the long term will require the fundamental re-think of some deeply ingrained managerial assumptions. Traditionally, we tend to consider workers as 'human tools' that the manager directs towards one task or another. In doing this, we lose most of the benefits to be gained from people's intelligence. In his disquieting indictment of Western management. Konosuke Matsushita—founder of one of Japan's largest companies—argues that:

> We [Japan] are going to win and the industrial West is going to lose out. There's not much you can do about it because the reasons of your failure are within yourselves. Your firms are, built on the Taylor model. Even worse, so are your heads. With your bosses doing the thinking while the workers wield the screw-drivers, you're convinced deep down that this is the right way to run a business. For you, the essence of management is getting the ideas out of the heads of the bosses and into the hands of labour.[20]

This must change. To do so, we must let on-the-job staff make their own choices about their work. This does not mean abandoning any notion of hierarchy, far from it. It means redefining our notion of management and leadership. The manager's role is to *lead*—that is, deciding which direction his or her group must go to follow the best business opportunities. The team is empowered to make decisions *within the scope of its work*. In practice, it means that it does not need to get management direction or approval every time a problem crops up, or an innovative thought is expressed. The team's responsibility is to find the best way to do the job, and this means using to its full potential the team's collective and individual intelligence.

Management's responsibility is to create the structures to support the teams in their work. The traditional pyramid must be turned upside down, and truly focused on its reason for being: *co-ordination of work*.

In this perspective, management competence can be seen as a *technology*. The technologies of organisation which have been created and described by numerous thinkers, from Adam Smith to Taiichi Ohno, must be understood and used as such: techniques and methods geared towards improving the co-ordination of people, machines and tasks. In this book, I have attempted to present the fundamental technologies of Business Process Re-engineering, and place them in the context of their main area of application: business processes. I hope that these techniques will help managers to face the new managerial challenge, and revitalise organisations to simultaneously increase both productivity and conviviality in the workplace.

GLOSSARY

◆

Bottleneck The slowest step of a process, where levels accumulate. It is usually possible to distinguish sequential steps in any process. The rate of flow varies from one step to the next. The slowest steps of the process will determine the flow rate of the entire process. Because upstream steps will flow faster, a bottleneck can be recognised by the accumulations it creates. In some cases, the bottleneck step can actually be far more efficient in terms of flow rates than any other step, yet, if too many flows converge towards that step, it still bottlenecks the entire process.

CEO Chief Executive Officer. The boss. This appellation is often used to distinguish the top job from the chairman, which, at least in Anglo-Saxon companies, has a different role from the managing director.

Command-and-control Traditional organisations tend to be built around the command-and-control idea. Such organisations are built around a strong hierarchical structure in which the role of the manager is to tell his or her subordinates what to do, and to control whether they are behaving according to company requirements. In short, the bosses think and the workers do. Such organisations will be held together by fairly constraining sets of procedures and internal regulations.
A typical command-and-control organisation will boast remote top management, mostly concerned with strategic planning, controlling middle-management, busy passing information downwards and playing career games and fairly uninvolved workers who will do as they're told and try to keep out of trouble.

Corporate culture change In vogue throughout the 1980s. The idea is to change 'corporate culture' in order to improve corporate results. The main difficulty is to agree upon what 'corporate culture' actually is. Everyone knows what it is when they are confronted with it but few can actually define it. All in all, it can be seen as the sum of behaviours people demonstrate in one particular company. These behaviours can usually be traced back to values, attitudes or policies. Corporate culture change tries to influence these fundamentals in the hope that the resulting behaviour will consequently change (for the better).
Some corporate culture change programmes have been spectacularly successful, others dismal failures and many indifferent. One can guess that

trying to modify people's values is fairly tricky in the first place. Furthermore, many such programmes often have purely motivational ends and pay little attention to operational realities. As a result, organisations which successfully motivate their staff to be more co-operative, customer-driven and proactive can still break down over technical process issues.

Cross functional management   Cross-functional management tries to bridge the gap between functional divisions by developing a new category of company-wide functions, managed by senior line managers—in addition to their functional responsibilities—to build a company-wide knowledge team in key areas. Cross-functional management tries to deal with the waste of time, effort and energy which arises from sequential hand-offs from one functional chimney to the next. Also, by early co-ordination of people from various functional departments, one can avoid unnecessary compatibility hassles further down the line. An extreme version of cross-functional management would be an organisation built exclusively along process lines as opposed to functional hierarchies.

Customer   What is meant here by 'customer' is the person who actually uses the product or service the supplier provides, as opposed to the 'client' who purchases the product or service. The customer is sometimes confused with the client. True, in many cases, client and customer are the same since the person who buys the product is also the one who uses it. However, in organisations, more often than not they are two distinct people. Purchasing departments usually buy for someone else in the organisation, as a mother will purchase a toy for her child. The customer may, or may not, have something to say about the purchase. In process terms it is important to distinguish customer from client because both might follow different aims: the client is likely to be more focused on price, while the customer is more interested in 'usability'.

Dependency   Dependency is what links one step to the next in a process: step A must be achieved for step B to occur. For instance, the key must be turned to unlock the door before the door can be opened. In several instances, real dependency becomes force of habit. Many people will turn the key in the lock before remembering they had left their door unlocked. Nonetheless, true dependency is often what holds a process together. Whenever we see that a dependency has disappeared, we can expect the process to change sooner or later. Some dependencies are kept hidden by territorial boundaries and processes become rather hard to understand unless a step back is taken and a more holistic approach identifies all the dependencies.

Dynamic models   A particular form of computer simulation which revolves around fast differential calculus. Dynamic models tend to reason in terms of accumulations (stocks) and rates (flows). These flows are regulated by a variety of rules which can be interdependent. Dynamic models are particularly useful to visualise dynamic behaviour in complex systems.

Empower   The fashionable answer to the command-and-control situation. In theory, to empower one's staff means to give employees the means to affect their jobs for increased results. In practice, it is often unclear how this can be achieved. Most 'empowering' recipes come down to the usual motherhoods about how to be a good boss and will have variable results according to who applies them. The empowerment issue is nonetheless both real and serious. How can we create organisations which valorise the competence, expertise and intuitions of their employees as opposed to trying to pin them down into narrow hierarchical roles?

Entrepreneurship   In brief: the qualities of the entrepreneur. Following Rosabeth Moss-Kanter's best-seller, *The Change Masters* (Routledge, 1983), corporate entrepreneurs (or intrapreneurs) were high in demand in the late 1980s. As another defence mechanism against the stultifying of large corporations, entrepreneurs are those managers who can negotiate, hijack or capture resources from the structure to nurture innovative projects which in turn will revitalise the entire organisation. As with many similar fads, intrapreneurship took a bit of a hit with the recession of the 1990s. The basic concept, however, remains sound, and entrepreneurs can be found here and there. No one, unfortunately, has as yet managed to train people to become entrepreneurs.

Excellence   Another business fad which originated from Tom Peters and Robert Waterman's *In Search of Excellence* (Harper & Row, 1982). On the basis of twenty-year averages of compound asset growth, compound equity growth, market value to book value ratio, return on capital, return on equity and return on sales, the authors identified 43 'excellent' companies. From these companies they derived a number of prescriptions. Excellence took a bit of a blow when it turned out that 5 years later only 12 of the original 43 had remained excellent and at least 8 were in serious trouble, but some of the precepts held and will pop up here and there once in a while. An excellent book nevertheless, the eight attributes of excellent companies are: (1) A bias for action; (2) close to the customer; (3) autonomy and entrepreneurship; (4) productivity through people; (5) hands-on, value driven; (6) stick to the knitting; (7) simple form, lean staff; (8) simultaneous loose-tight properties.

Exponential growth or decay   Exponential growth (or decay) happens when a quantity will double (halve) itself at regular intervals. Exponential growth is typically associated with population growth curves. In general, it can be fairly surprising since the numbers stay small for a long time and then suddenly become outrageously large. For instance, take a piece of paper and fold it in half. You have just doubled it thickness. Fold it in half again and it is now four times its original thickness. Supposing you could fold the paper about 40 times, the resulting pile would be high enough to reach the moon!

Facilitator   The facilitator is someone who plays a particular role in group dynamics: their only concern is the process, not the result of the working session. A good facilitator remains indifferent to the issue at hand and will help the group resolve it by establishing ground rules, holding the group to these rules, and in practice, controlling expression time.

Feedback loops   Feedback loops represent circular causality. In most things we do, we tend to assume a linear causality of the type 'I open the door'. In actual fact, the door has an effect on me, since it tells me how much pressure to apply, and for how long. The feedback represents the return of information in a system. Feedback loops are a way of representing situations where A influences B, which in turn influences A:

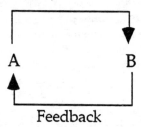

Feedback

Forrester effect   Named after Jay Forrester, who first described it, the Forrester effect occurs when small variations at one end of a process result in very wide variations at the other end. This typically occurs in production/distribution processes where small market variations can trigger massive changes at production scheduling level. This amplification effect happens due to the communication delays between one link in the supply chain to the next.

Hand-offs   Hand-offs happen every time a file or a product changes hands in an organisation. Hand-offs are seen by BPR zealots as the source of all evils, since at each hand-off, work is typically (1) stalled in an out-pile; (2) moved around; (3) stalled in an in-pile. Furthermore, hand-offs also create breaks in the information flow with all the dire consequences this implies: who ever tells the next person down the line everything they need to know? Hand-offs are particularly noxious when they happen between separate departments (for instance, a dossier has to move from finance to sales) since they tend to involve vertical (I'll pass it on to my boss, who'll give it to yours, and then your boss can pass it down to you) as well as lateral hand-offs.

Implementation board   A board which can be kept either on paper or on a wall to help project managers keep track of things. The board can look something like this:

ACTION	OWNER	BY WHEN	CHECK-UP	COM-MENTS
A brief description of the action	Who is supposed to make it happen	Deadline	An appointment to check how things are going before the deadline	Comments
Action 1	Sylvia	15/6/95	5/6/95	
Action 2	Peter	16/6/95	4/6/95	

Improvement killers   Little, apparently innocent, comments which can stop any improvement dead in its tracks. These comments will typically sound like: 'It's not possible'; 'It's not our job'; 'It shouldn't be like this'; 'The answer is obvious'; 'I'm already doing it'; 'I'll do it tomorrow' and so on. To be fought ruthlessly.

Interface   Technically, the boundary between two different substances. Here, we mean the meeting points between different territories or areas. Interfaces hide dependencies. For instance, when crossing from one county to the next, a major road can turn into a small, winding track, before becoming a large road again. At the interface of the two counties, no one is interested in doing anything about this road—it's the other side's job. However, the traffic dependency between the two is very real as all those who get caught in the endless traffic jams will tell you.

Inventory   Inventory is basically what you hold in stock—whether materials, work-in-progress or finished goods. Inventory can also mean the monetary value of this stock. One practical way of thinking about inventory is to consider that it represents all the money the firm has invested in purchasing things which it intends to sell.* Inventory is the headache of most people who try to streamline operations because it represents the fat

* See Goldratt, E & Cox, J (1984) *The Goal*, Gower, Aldershot.

in the system. Inventory-free operation is one of the aims of just-in-time management.

IT Information technology—everything which revolves around using computers. To the enthusiast, IT represents the third (or is it fourth?) industrial revolution. To the cynics, IT is the biggest snake-oil con of the century. Like it or not, information technology has invaded every aspect of working life—sometimes forcibly. However, as we begin to evaluate the returns on the massive IT investments pursued since World War II there are rumours that we might be facing a diminishing returns situation. IT is not the panacea it seemed to be. It is tremendously useful at dealing with repetitive, frequent tasks, but most attempts at getting IT to do more sophisticated things can be questioned. Handle with care.

JIT Just-in-time. Originally developed by Taiichi Ohno as the Toyota Production System (he never called it anything else), JIT came to mean a generic production system built on a pull (only produce from orders) rather than a push (produce and stockpile, regardless of what is ordered) production principle. JIT is mostly presented in the many ways it differs from traditional production systems. In fact, Ohno's original thinking seemed to have evolved around the concept of production cells (the famous U-shaped production units). Within the cells, production happens part-by-part, with no work-in-progress inventory, and flexible arrangements to modulate work according to demand. The cells are connected with each other by the kanban system which controls the movement of small-parts lots of uniform size.

Kaizen A term coined by Masaaki Imai to signify continuous improvement. The underlying intuition behind kaizen is that most innovative productivity leaps will slide back through sloppiness or sheer entropy unless they are followed up by constant small-step improvements. Kaizen represents the small-step improvement strategy which is often opposed to Western-style big leap actions.

Kanban Originally a Japanese word for card, which came to represent a production scheduling system. The kanban system links visually the units within a pull production system, each order being represented by a kanban card. With this system, the downstream process gets parts from the upstream process. Upstream produces the quantity removed by the following process. Kanban can be used for inventory control by reducing the number of cards in operation. On a warning note: production quantities need to be levelled for the system to operate effectively.

Kill-date A termination tag which should be placed on each new process as it is implemented. It is a practical way to avoid sedimentation of layers of old processes which are constantly amended and added upon until the entire workflow simply gets bogged down.

Lead-time   Lead-time can mean a number of things. Traditionally, it represents the span of time spent between placing an order and receiving the corresponding delivery. Here, we extend that notion to the time it takes to complete one individual product from start to finish. In traditional systems, lead-time is moderately important as long as one uniform product is produced frequently—who cares how long this same product actually took to be produced. In diversified production, where each item becomes individualised, the production time for each individual product becomes critically important. In this work, I have taken lead-times as a simple measure of process effectiveness.

Lean enterprise   Coined by James Womack and Daniel Jones in *The Machine that Changed the World* (Macmillan, 1990), the lean enterprise consists of a company which would operate along the principles of lean (ie inventory-free) production. Progressively taken to represent the fast, flexible, focused, empowered, cross-functional firms that managers will dream of until the turn of the century.

Lean production   A generic name for the Toyota Production System. It encapsulates more or less all the aspects of Toyota's industrial advances from shop-floor management to employment policy or product development lead-times. Lean production tends to have a connotation of 'waste reduction', mostly inspired by Taiichi Ohno's constant war against wastage in any form.

Limiting factor   In any system, it is important to realise that the most important factor at any one time is the most limiting one. In a way, the most limiting factor is the bottleneck. Limiting factors, however, are not localised. For instance, one factor can be limiting one moment and not the next. In baking bread, the most limiting factor can be adding yeast to the flour—no amount of additional flour will help without yeast. Yet at the next stage, the most limiting factor could be oven temperature. If the oven is not hot enough, the bread won't bake, no matter how long it stays in there and so forth. Limiting factors are not necessarily quantitatively important, so they tend to be dismissed. Bad mistake.

One-minute-managing   Yet another management fad. This one was triggered by Kenneth Blanchard and Spencer Johnson's remarkable little book, *The One Minute Manager* (William Morrow, 1982) on setting goals, praising and blaming people. The idea is that these fundamental managerial tasks can all be conducted in exactly one minute, which largely accounts for its fantastic success among Western managers. At the end of the day, the book puts simply and plainly the behavioural techniques of the carrot-and-stick approach which underlies much of managerial roles. The original book led to the other 'one-minute' titles, and as a whole they can be considered as the one-minute managing approach.

Ostrich strategy   Whenever a problem appears, stick your head in the sand and wait for it to go away. If no sand is available, a brown paper bag will do the trick.

Output   Output is what is produced by a process: what comes out of the last step. Output generally means the physical production of the process, but it can also be understood as the financial or intellectual production of the process. In designing measures for production systems, Goldratt proposes the interesting notion of throughput: the rate at which the system generates money through sales.* Throughput makes an interesting contrast with output, since most process managers tend to be obsessed with the latter and could benefit greatly from giving a little more thought to the former.

Paradigm shift   Paradigm is a term created by Thomas Kuhn to represent the set of assumptions, questions and answers which prevail in the scientific community at a given time. It has often been extended to the notion of 'managerial paradigm', meaning the set of assumptions, tools and techniques which represent managerial know-how at a point in time. According to Kuhn, such paradigms can shift in rather sudden and brutal revolutions when disconfirming evidence accumulates to the point of critical mass.

Parallel processing   Some dependencies between process steps are not always necessary. They can exist for convenience or by force of habit. These steps can then be uncoupled and processed in parallel: ie independently and at the same time. Parallel processing is one of the most effective time-winning strategies in complex processes.

Pareto's Law   Twenty per cent of the causes explain eighty per cent of the effects. Often verifiable but hard to prove. It is unclear whether the economist Vilfredo Pareto actually formulated such a law. As far as I can tell, the closest he got to it was to suggest that 20 per cent of the population will always control the remaining 80 per cent. If anyone knows more about how the 80/20 rule came to be known as Pareto's Law, please let me know.

Post-it notes   Mostly yellow small sticky papers developed by 3M. They are at the heart of one of the most famous legends about the creative use of mistakes. Someone at 3M, so the story goes, developed an embarrassing glue that wouldn't actually glue. Some creative thinking created a need nobody

---

* See Goldratt, E and Cox, J (1984) *The Goal*, Gower, Aldershot.

had ever thought of before: paper that only sticks a bit! In team-based work, post-it notes are a key part of the kit.

Process A sequence of dependent events. In practice, almost anything which involves time can be called a process under some form or other. The definition is both incomplete and arbitrary, but will have to do. In particular, a process should also be understood to include various parallel branches which will link up at one step. From a modelling point of view, a process can easily be represented by stocks (accumulations) and flows.

Process map A drawing of the process sequence where each step is represented by a box and the sequence is represented by arrows. Process maps also include feedback loops, where the sequence falls back on itself and certain steps have to be repeated. A key tool in process redesign.

Pull system A pull system is any process controlled by the downstream steps: demand pulls products through the process, as opposed to a push system where offer pushes the products through. A pull system can be created anywhere one reverses the demand/offer mechanisms.

Quality circles A generic term used to describe worker work-groups in improvement efforts. Quality circles became very popular in the 1980s when it became apparent that Japanese firms were benefiting extensively from worker suggested improvements. Unfortunately, most quality circle experiments failed in the West. Many reasons were proposed to explain this failure, most having to do with culture in some form or other. It is true that traditional shop-floor environments were very ill-suited for the kind of work quality circles imply. However, it is also apparent that quality circles are, in Japan, the result of 30 years of experimentation and learning on worker involvement. Thus it is quite unlikely that adopting the technique without making the effort of going through the learning curve is going to pay off right away. A touchy subject with many Total Quality experts.

Quality revolution Putting a good face on Japan's industrial lesson to the West: quality matters. While the West was busy with mass production and using in-built obsolescence on customers, a few Japanese firms were religiously applying the teaching of American quality consultants such as Deming or Juran. We all know what happened next: better products at a lower cost. Once the point had been made forcibly enough, most Western firms decided to go all the way on quality, and some succeeded. Moreover, the quality ideology became so successful it even reached the corridors of political power and became institutionalised in the form of the ISO norms of dark renown. The quality movement has been increasingly criticised for, as revolutions are wont to do, turning into a bureaucratic exercise which has very little to do with quality.

R&D   Research and development. Traditionally, R&D mostly concerned products—how to improve them, or develop new ones. Cross-functional management is largely trying to change that and integrate both marketing and production into research and development. The idea is to develop new products that will be easy to produce and fast to market. Time is of the essence in markets where new products appear every six months. In practice, the major change this shift imposes on development is the reduction of part references: using as many standard parts as possible for developing new products.

Rouge complex   Ford's megalomaniac dream. Standardisation was one of Ford's industrial discoveries. In order to produce cheap cars, he needed standardised parts from his suppliers to push through his own assembly plants using his production system. The result was an enormous integrated industrial complex at Rouge, near Detroit, which was not much better than the 'Dark Satanic Mills' of an earlier period.

Span of control   Throughout the 1960s, the idea progressively emerged from psychological studies that a manager could not successfully manage more than six to nine people. This 'span of control' theory spread rapidly, and although evidence to the contrary is historically overwhelming, it will still reappear in management discussions.

Standardisation   One of Henry Ford's key insights. Standardisation of work, parts and processes is a prerequisite for mass production. In pre-Ford workshops, parts were not standardised so that each part had to be worked on to fit with the next. By standardising parts, Ford could produce faster and more reliably. Very soon he realised that the same applied to working practices and processes. Standardisation remains a crucial concern for any industrial system.

Taylorism   Frederick Taylor's notion of scientific organisation of work. Pushing the idea of division and specialisation of labour to the extreme, Taylor tried to optimise tasks (ie how large should a shovel be for the worker to shovel the most dirt in the least time). This idea of 'optimisation' or in Taylor's terms the 'one best way' was massively successful in terms of productivity. Unfortunately, it had many tragic downsides in terms of worker alienation. Taylor has the infamous honour of being hated both in his own time, and by posterity. Apart from being a difficult character by all accounts, in his time he was hated by the bosses because his system changed so fundamentally the productivity equation that (1) one had to use it to remain competitive and (2) it permitted spectacular increases in workers' wages. He was hated by the labour side because the system virtually destroyed the worker organisation of the time by enabling individual workers to sell their work directly to the factory. Over time, Taylor became associated with all the abuses conducted in his name in large factories, until well into the 1970s.

In the light of what has happened since, it seems that Taylor's main mistake was to apply his engineering assumption to working practices; engineers who knew all about optimising machines could now optimise worker's movements. Of course, this implicit assumption of treating people as machines would have all the dire consequences we now face. Unfortunately, this mindset still lurks in many managerial settings.

Team talk   A group warm-up technique. Team talk is actually different from 'conversation'. Conversation is what we naturally do when we talk to one another: we express verbally what goes through our mind. It's usually not particularly ordered, and most of the fun comes out of arguing a point or kidding each other. The aim of team talk is to convey information to the group without getting entangled in the social dimension, Team talk is not used all the time but only at specific moments when things have to get cleared up before 'normal' conversation can resume. The rules are (1) everybody speaks in turn; (2) people state what they want to say without expecting any immediate reaction from the others; (3) others listen and do not reply; (4) conversation starts only when everyone has had their say.

Trigger point   A trigger point is a signal in a process which activates the next step. It can be a computerised order, an empty box or a card in a kanban system, or someone yelling for a report from across the room. In complex processes, trigger points can also be linked to 'critical mass'. At a certain stage, the accumulation is such that something has to give, and the system itself can be changed as a result.

TQM   Total quality management. According to the experts, 'Total Quality is an umbrella term which includes: everything that an organisation does to determine whether its customers return to them and recommend them to others; minimising costs through efficient and effective organisation; maximising the resources of the workforce to co-operate in making the company the best in the field; and finally, the exploitation of the weaknesses of the company's rivals'.* I gather that TQM is the management of all this.

Value-added   The value which is actually added to the product or service by an operation. Another way of looking at it is the work that a customer would legitimately be happy to pay for because he or she would see how that benefits him or her. Surprisingly little of what companies do is value-added. Marketing, Finance, Business Strategy etc, add very little value to

---

* Hutchins, D (1992) *Achieve Total Quality*, Directors Books, Hemel Hempstead.

the product or service your company is providing. The role of most of these (rather expensive) functions is either to help the company sell more, control its operations and people, or make a quick buck on the money market. How would customers feel if they realised that at least 10p of every £1 they pay at purchase goes to people whose job is to convince them, the customer, to buy more of the product?

Variability   Nothing ever happens exactly the same way twice. Variability is the slight difference which occurs within a repetitive action from one go to the next. Usually, these variations happen around a mean average. The breadth of these variations is the variability in the operation. Variability is a key element of quality since it is linked to standardisation and reliability.

Zero investment   A key improvement rule. As Taiichi Ohno was fond of saying, 'Use your ideas, not your money!' Confronted with the need for improvement, most people's reaction is of the 'more is better' type: we need more resources, more time, more people, more machines etc. A zero investment constraint focuses the mind wonderfully on finding a clever way to solve the problem. This rule need not be followed absolutely and blindly, most improvement activities will need some resources to get off the ground. Yet it remains a sound general principle to focus a redesign group on drawing waste out of the system, not adding more resources.

REFERENCES

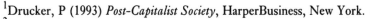

[1] Drucker, P (1993) *Post-Capitalist Society*, HarperBusiness, New York.

[2] Stalk, G & Hout, T (1990) *Competing Against Time*, Free Press, New York.

[3] CSC Index (1994) *Où en est le Reengineering*.

[4] 'Re-engineering Europe', *The Economist*, Feb 26 1994.

[5] S. Womack, J, Jones, D and Roos, D (1990) *The Machine that Changed the World*, Macmillan, New York.

[6] Smith, A (1776) *The Wealth of Nations*, Everyman's Library, London.

[7] Taylor, F (1911) *The Principles of Scientific Management*, Harper & Brothers, New York.

[8] Hammer, M & Champy, J (1993) *Reengineering the Corporation*, Harper Collins, New York.

[9] Imai, M (1986) *Kaizen*, McGraw-Hill, New York.

[10] Dimancescu, D (1992) *The Seamless Enterprise*, HarperBusiness, New York.

[11] Jaques, E (1989) *Requisite Organisations*, Cason Hall, New York.

[12] Rehfeld, J (1991) 'What working for a Japanese company taught me,' *Accurate Business Forecasting*, *Harvard Business Review*, Boston.

[13] BCG (1993) *Re-engineering and beyond: A Senior Management Perspective*.

[14] Forrester, J (1961) *Industrial Dynamics*, Productivity Press, Cambridge.

[15] Lester Thurow is quoted in Davenport, T (1993), *Process Innovation*, Harvard Business School Press, Boston.

[16] Davenport, T (1993) *Process Innovation*, Harvard Business School Press, Boston *ibid.*

[17] de Geus, A (1988) 'Planning as learning', *Harvard Business Review*, March/April 1988, 70–74.

[18] Classe, A (1994) *Software Tools for Re-engineering*, a Business Intelligence report. If you are interested in the full report, contact David Harvey at Business Intelligence, Forum House, 1 Graham Road, London SW19 3SW.

[19] Quoted in Champy, J & Hammer, M *op cit.*

[20] Quoted in Pascale, R (1990) *Managing on the Edge*, Simon & Schuster, New York.

INDEX